Washington
Past and Present

A Guide to the Nation's Capital

The United States Capitol Historical Society
Washington, D.C.
1987

STAFF FOR THE SECOND EDITION

Donald R. Kennon, Richard Striner, *Authors*
Robert L. Breeden, *Editorial Director*
Paul D. Martin, *Editor*
Cynthia B. Scudder, *Art Director*
Pat Lanza Field, *Illustrations Editor*
Ruth L. Connor, *Researcher*
Richard M. Crum, *Picture Legend Writer*
Barbara Bricks, Elizabeth W. Fisher, *Staff Assistants*
Robert W. Messer, *Production Manager*
Malvina B. Lester, *Indexer*

Right: *Jogger rims the Tidal Basin under a canopy of Cherry blossoms,* (Adam Woolfitt) Cover: *Capitol Building, Washington Monument; and Lincoln Memorial symbolize the proud heritage of a nation (T. Stephen Thompson);* UNIPHOTO, Endpapers; *Stars and Stripes wave free at the Washington Monument;* (William Douthitt) Preceding pages; *Gen. Andrew Jackson raises his hat in salute in Lafayette Park opposite the White House.* (Williams S. Weems, Woodfin Camp, Inc.) Contents page: *Sky rockets light up the Capitol during Bicentennial festivities. (Martin Ickow. UNIPHOTO).*

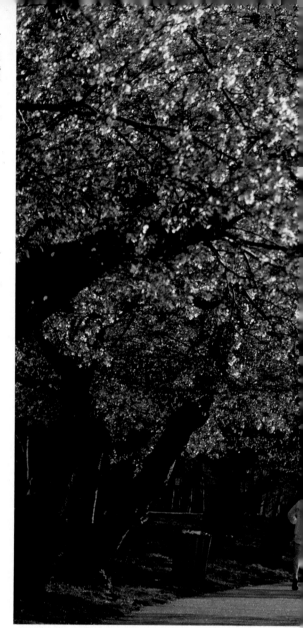

Foreword

Washington is an inspiration to people the world over. The memorials here, said India's Prime Minister Nehru, "are the real temples to which each generation must pay tribute and, in doing so, must catch something of the fire that burnt in the hearts of those who were the torch bearers of freedom not only for this country, but for the world."

Full of interesting insights into the history of America, this book is foremost about Washington, D.C. Built for the people, this

city has been the central stage of America's dramatic past and is the take-off point for her challenging future. As one historian has written, "The story of the capital's creation—like that of the nation itself—is one of daring experiment and noble compromise, salted with acts of greed and deceit." That statement will be appreciated by all who understand our nation's troubled birth. As Carl Sandburg once said, "Whenever a people or an institution forgets its early hard beginnings it is beginning to decay."

The U. S. Capitol Historical Society presents this book in the hope that with it,

visitors and potential visitors to Washington will more fully understand and appreciate this great city. The book contains more than 150 illustrations selected from public and private collections to document the city's growth. The text covers the full history of the city and includes many fascinating anecdotes. In addition to being a history, the book is an excellent guide to present-day Washington. The visitor to our nation's capital can be proud to own this volume.

Fred Schwengel

Fred Schwengel
President, U.S. Capitol Historical Society

Contents

Introduction

Little more than a century ago, Frederick Douglass called Washington, D.C., "the most luminous point of American territory; a city recently transformed and made beautiful in its body and in its spirit." He spoke at the unveiling of the Freedmen's Monument in Lincoln Park. He was moved not only by the capital's spiritual transformation in the wake of slavery's abolition, but also by its physical transformation in anticipation of the Centennial. Nevertheless, the physical reality of Washington in 1876 presents a stark contrast to the Washington of today.

Visitors to the nation's capital might think that the city was born beautiful, since it focuses on memorials to Presidents and military heroes, a maze of statuary, parks large and small, and great public buildings, especially the White House, the Capitol, and the Supreme Court. But as this book reveals, the city evolved slowly and painfully from the raw and graceless town that Dickens decried in 1842 as the "City of Magnificent Intentions." For much of its history, it was dirty and discomforting; its few aesthetically pleasing buildings and monuments served as a contrast which emphasized the surrounding blight.

When Abraham Lincoln came to Washington from Illinois in 1861, only a few scattered buildings lay in the swamp between the Executive Mansion and Capitol Hill, and the unfinished stub of the Washington Monument rose in a pasture where cattle grazed. The domeless Capitol and the half-built monument were twin symbols of the unfinished agenda of a young nation embarked on a difficult journey—an experiment in self-government—begun a century earlier. Despite the Civil War, Lincoln was determined to complete the dome of the Capitol, sure in his knowledge that "We live by symbols," as Mr. Justice Holmes later observed. As the dome moved toward completion, it was a symbol of the unity that Lincoln struggled to preserve.

From the west entrance of the Capitol, one can stand today and see the Reflecting Pool, and a mile away the Washington Monument, not completed until 1884. It would be impossible to catalog all the great events that have taken place within the Capitol's marble walls, but any list would include the great debates in Congress, when Daniel Webster, Henry Clay, and John Calhoun held their colleagues spellbound. It would include landmark decisions of the Supreme Court, delivered by its Justices from early cramped quarters in the basement of the Capitol, and later from the impressive room near the present Senate Chamber—before the Court was appropriately housed, in 1935, in its present magnificent building.

This book traces Washington's jagged and often turbulent development from its feeble beginning to the public magnificence that we enjoy today. Few cities equal Washington in its cultural wealth—its theaters and museums, its galleries filled with great works donated by citizens. We can each take pride in the beauty of the capital, for much progress has been achieved in making it a full embodiment of the aspirations of the American people, a people often in disagreement over means and methods, but united in the never-ending quest for liberty, equal opportunity, and equal justice under law.

Warren E. Burger
Former Chief Justice of the United States

Washington Past:
The City That History Made

By Donald R. Kennon

"This embryo capital, where Fancy sees
Squares in morasses, obelisks in trees..."
Thomas Moore, Irish Poet

Even through the mist that March morning in 1791, Maj. Pierre Charles L'Enfant could see squares in morasses, obelisks in trees—and more—as a grand vista of broad avenues radiating from stately public buildings took shape in this brilliant Frenchman's imagination. Though the area destined to become the nation's permanent capital was partly swamp and underbrush, L'Enfant relished the opportunity to design a capital city out of a wilderness "on such a scale as to leave room for that aggrandizement and embellishment which the increase of the wealth of the nation will permit it to pursue at any period however remote."

Trained as an architect and engineer, L'Enfant was familiar with European capitals such as Paris and London, yet he rejected their example in order to create a new and original plan. The capital of the new United States of America would express the youth, exuberance, and boundless potential of the nation and its people. Moreover, as the seat of government it would reflect the governing principles of the Constitution—a new capital for the new nation.

Conceived in rebellion, delivered through turmoil and war, the United States of America began its existence as a conscious experiment in self-government—mankind's "last, best hope" as Abraham Lincoln would observe. Prior to 1787 the young nation was but a loose confederation; primary ties of loyalty were to local centers of power—town, county, state. Concentrated power was feared. Prevailing opinion stressed the weakness of human nature and the ease with which moral integrity and public order could be subverted. The Constitution of 1787 was designed to overcome these problems through checks and balances and the separation of powers. The Constitution was a blueprint for the new government; the planning and creation of the capital would express the same grand design.

Like the Constitution, the selection of a site for the permanent national capital was the result of compromise. To obtain Thomas Jefferson's support for the federal assumption of state debts—a key point in his plan to increase federal authority—Alexander Hamilton agreed to the principle of a southern capital. Under the terms of the Residence Act of 1790, Congress would meet in Philadelphia until 1800 while the capital city was being readied. Three commissioners chosen to oversee the location of the capital promptly named the city "Washington" in honor of the first President.

President Washington, whose home, Mount Vernon, was on the Virginia side of the Potomac, supervised the site selection.

Statue of George Washington flanks a painting of the signers of the Declaration of Independence in the Capitol Rotunda. Soldier turned statesman, Washington guided the capital city through its early stages, from determining its location to overseeing its design, funding, and construction.

PAT LANZA FIELD

Though criticized for the financial gain he might realize from the selection of a site so close to his home, Washington decided on the area that today forms the District of Columbia and Alexandria, Virginia. He then chose Andrew Ellicott of Maryland and his talented, self-taught black assistant, Benjamin Banneker, to survey the "ten-mile square," a 100-square-mile tract. Finally, Washington named the idealistic young Frenchman, Pierre L'Enfant, chief engineer.

To look at the plan for the capital that L'Enfant presented in 1791 is to see the new government as conceived by the men who ran it. Like overlapping spider webs, street patterns mesh together several separate focal points. Corresponding to the three branches of the new government—executive, legislative, and judicial—the plan's three main focal centers were separated, but linked by

10

*P*astoral setting for a fledgling capital: Rolling hills of Georgetown command a panoramic view of the Potomac River in an idyllic engraving of the capital area published in 1801. On the river a merchant ship makes for Georgetown wharves. British furniture and luxury goods exchanged for colonial tobacco brought London elegance to the small port community. Buildings along the point of land curving beyond Mason's Island, at center right, hug the waterfront of early Washington. The capital city would gradually grow to fill the entire District of Columbia.

avenues of communication. The area's highest elevation, Jenkins' Hill—"a pedestal waiting for a monument" according to L'Enfant—was reserved for Congress and the Capitol. The executive department, a mile and a half to the northwest, was to be centered on the President's House, a "palace" L'Enfant called it. The third branch, the judicial, was to be placed somewhere between the President's Palace and the Capitol, away from the major avenues, unconnected and presumably uninfluenced by either of the other branches.

The city L'Enfant planned was an open community, one intended to be accessible—to link the governors with the governed. Although subsequently altered and modified, L'Enfant's plan would in time create a capital fulfilling the grand vision of the city's founders. But very little of this vision of grandeur was evident when the government arrived to set up house in November of 1800. L'Enfant himself was gone, dismissed in 1792 for several arrogant actions, including

pulling down a house belonging to a cousin of City Commissioner Daniel Carroll.

Access to the capital was still limited and difficult. There were few roads to link Washington with the outside world. First Lady Abigail Adams once wandered in the woods for two hours returning from Baltimore before a vagabond appeared, as she recalled, "to extricate us out of our difficulty." Still more morass and trees than squares and obelisks, Washington was aptly described as "neither town nor village," a city which, according to one congressman, "so many are willing to come to and all so anxious to leave."

Why were the high hopes of the capital's founders unrealized? Part of the explanation is simple—not enough money. The city lacked an economic base, efforts to improve the port facilities of Georgetown and Alexandria notwithstanding. President Washington and the commissioners of the federal city counted upon land speculation to finance construction. Expecting the capital to attract an influx of business and

*H*andkerchief map (below) records the vision of the federal city's major planners, Frenchman Pierre L'Enfant, portrayed at right, and George Washington, who at left reviews a survey of the city with his wife, Martha, and her grandchildren. L'Enfant's plan for the capital stressed radial boulevards, parks, and spacious vistas. The city's founders, drawing on the beauty of Renaissance and classical styles, created a masterpiece—the world's first national capital established by law and comprehensively planned prior to construction.

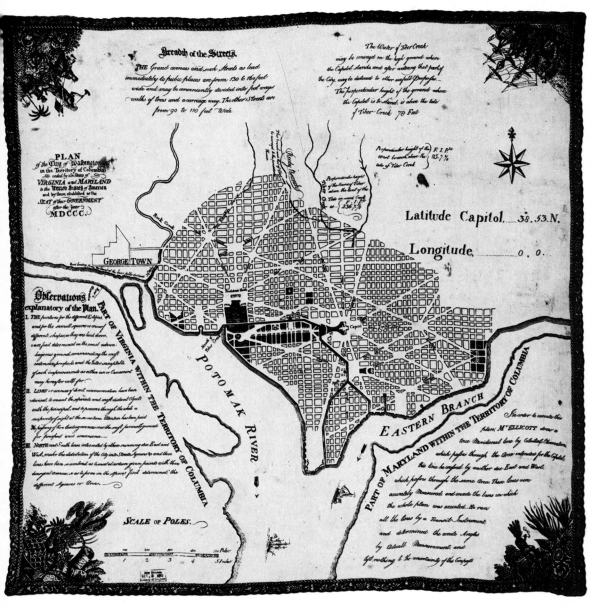

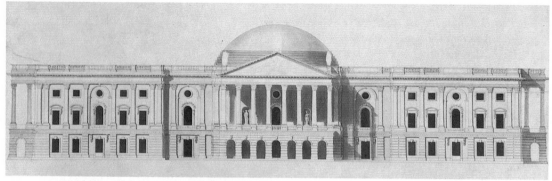

Masonic apron girds President George Washington (opposite) as he lays the cornerstone of the U.S. Capitol on September 18, 1793. A silver plate on the foundation under the cornerstone marked the date as the 13th year of American independence, the first year of Washington's second term, and the year of Masonry 5793. Masonic ceremonies also accompanied the laying of the cornerstones for the District and for the White House. Physician William Thornton (left) won a contest for the design of the Capitol. Thornton's plan (above) impressed Washington with its "Grandeur, Simplicity, and Convenience."

population, the commissioners offered lots at public auction. Masking the area's true nature—Goose Creek was renamed the Tiber and Jenkins' Hill became Capitoline Hill—did not help. Only 35 lots were sold at the first auction. A second auction was no more successful; by 1800 less than one-tenth of the lots had been sold. Only when Congress and the state of Maryland came to the rescue with financial assistance was work able to continue.

Design of the Capitol Building and the President's House went more smoothly. Plans ranging from the grotesquely absurd to the sedately classical were submitted to the two architectural competitions established by City Commissioners Thomas Johnson, Daniel Carroll, and David Stuart. An Irish architect living in South Carolina, James

Hoban, won the competition for the President's residence with his design for a Palladian-style mansion. Dr. William Thornton, physician and amateur architect, entered the Capitol competition late, but won easily with a plan Thomas Jefferson found "simple, noble, beautiful, excellently distributed, and moderate in size."

Left in the lurch, however, was the Supreme Court. A separate home for the Court, as proposed by L'Enfant, was not to come about until 1935. Until then it was left to fend for itself, a poor orphan seeking shelter within the confines of the Capitol.

Design, as L'Enfant could attest, was one thing; construction was another. Finances continued to be a problem. One imaginative but impractical supervisor of public buildings, Samuel Blodgett, held two lotteries

*B*ritish Rear Adm. Sir George Cockburn
(above) strikes a conqueror's pose while
Washington burns during the War of 1812. At
right, Redcoats under his command torch public
buildings. Cockburn's fleet sailed up the
Patuxent River and landed troops that entered
the ill-defended capital at dusk on August 24,
1814. By next nightfall the city lay in ruins.
Fire-scarred and crumbling, the White House
(below, at right) stands desolate opposite St.
John's Church in Lafayette Square.

—first prize a "superb hotel with baths, out-houses, etc."—which were no more success-ful than land auctions in raising revenue. If lack of money was a problem, equally dis-tressing was the lack of skilled labor. The commissioners' attempt to recruit workmen in Europe failed. For unskilled labor, slaves were hired from the owners of plantations throughout Maryland and Virginia. Ironi-cally, the capital of "the land of the free" was built in part by slave labor.

Construction of the city proceeded slowly. Work on the President's House was suspended so that the Capitol could be readied in time for Congress' arrival. When the government did arrive in 1800, it found a collection of shantytowns surrounding the unfinished Capitol and White House, sepa-rated by a vast expanse of uncleared swamp. Cattle grazed on the Mall, snakes slithered through unfinished houses, hogs rooted in trash heaps, and mosquitoes bred in an un-completed canal. The only commercial estab-lishment was a brewery, and just 372 dwell-ings were found habitable—"most of them small miserable huts," reported one cabinet

*F*irst native-American architect to oversee construction of the Capitol, Charles Bulfinch (left) succeeded Benjamin Latrobe in 1818 and completed the job of rebuilding the British-pillaged structure. Bulfinch modified the original design of the central section, including the Rotunda and the dome. His efforts appear below in the earliest known photograph of the Capitol Building, taken in 1846. Bulfinch's copper-sheathed central dome arches higher than the original, planned by William Thornton in 1793 but never built. Today the central portion of the West Front of the Capitol remains as the only visible exterior remnant of the Bulfinch design.

member—for a population of 500 families plus 300 members of the government.

Washington remained a small provincial city from 1800 to 1830. Grand predictions of growth, such as William Thornton's confident expectation of a population of 160,000 in a few years, proved greatly exaggerated. The capital's only business was government. During the Jeffersonian era the federal government remained small, and consequently the city remained small. In 1802 the government establishment in Washington numbered only 291 persons, 138 of whom were congressmen. By 1829 government personnel had grown to but 625, of whom 273 were congressmen. The only department with more than a handful of employees was the Treasury Department, which then included the Postal Service.

Though the city's population (exclusive of Georgetown and Alexandria) increased from slightly more than 3,000 in 1800 to nearly 19,000 by 1830, its rate of growth was below the national average and considerably less than that of other major urban areas. The rate of growth in the black community, a significant portion of the population, rose proportionately faster—from just over 700 slaves and free blacks in 1800 to more than 5,000 by 1830.

Other than government personnel, and the slaves and free blacks who formed the city's unskilled labor pool, what kinds of people were drawn to Washington? Observers were unanimous: The city seemed to attract society's outcasts. The poor, "straggling vagabond beggars, which the seat of government draws together"; would-be office-holders, "a class of swaggering sycophants"; and other misfits seeking redress or revenge descended upon a city with few jobs to offer. The result was not a pretty sight. "The people are poor," one critic noted, "and live like fishes, by eating each other." Since most property was government-owned and therefore tax-exempt, the city had little revenue to spend on jails or relief for the poor. Rather than a national showplace, Washington had become a national embarrassment. Yet some semblance of order was becoming evident.

Iron ribs exposed amid construction cranes, the present-day Capitol's tiered crown takes shape during the Civil War years (top). Designed by Thomas U. Walter, the completed nine-million-pound cast-iron dome (above) replaced Bulfinch's structure and formed a gleaming pedestal for the 7½-ton bronze Statue of Freedom, bolted into place in 1863.

Under the enlarged city charter of 1804 two public schools were opened in 1806. The Capitol's two wings were completed and joined by a wooden passageway by 1810. Pennsylvania Avenue was improved and work was resumed on the White House. Then just as Washington was beginning to show some promise, the War of 1812 brought havoc to the capital. L'Enfant's open city proved to be militarily indefensible. In August of 1814 a British force commanded by Rear Adm. Sir George Cockburn routed American defenders at Bladensburg, Maryland, and marched into the capital on the heels of the fleeing government. The night of the 24th the British set fire to the city's major public buildings, in retribution for the burning of York, Canada, by American troops. The Capitol and the White House were left standing as gutted shells.

At war's end it seemed certain the time had come for the government to move. Congress, however, voted by a thin margin to remain in Washington, impressed by the offer of the city's bankers to finance reconstruction. President Madison took up residence in the Octagon House, and Congress met for a time in the Patent Office and then in a simple brick building constructed by private citizens. Adversity had welded the governing community and the city together, prompting Washingtonian Thomas Law to poetry: "And the new edifice in splendor sprung, Like a Phoenix from its ashes."

As the capital was rebuilt following the war, more and more of L'Enfant's grand design became apparent. If public squares still masqueraded as morasses, and trees still hid obelisks from view, the government at least had adapted to the city. The executive

The President's House (left) faces unpaved Pennsylvania Avenue in a scene from around 1810. The Executive Mansion evolved from plans drawn in 1792 by Irish-born architect James Hoban (above). Thomas Jefferson held the first public reception in the mansion in 1801. Popular President Andrew Jackson drew a boisterous crowd to his inaugural celebration in 1829 (below).

Benjamin Harrison's grandson guides his pet goat.

Guest bedroom displays Victorian decor.

Archie Roosevelt, with brother Quentin, salutes Theodore Roosevelt's White House police.

Crowd gathers for Calvin Coolidge's annual New Year's Day open house.

Herbert Hoover, with

William Howard Taft greets socialites.

Sheep crop the south lawn during World War I.

wife, Lou, entertains disabled veterans on south lawn.

branch was indeed clustered around the President's House, and congressmen segregated themselves in boardinghouse societies around the Capitol Building.

Viewing this arrangement, one foreign visitor in the 1820s wondered: "The plan marked out for this metropolis of the empire, is gigantic, and the public buildings, whether in progress or design, bear all the stamp of grandeur. How many centuries shall pass away ere the clusters of little villages, now scattered over this plain, shall assume the form and magnificence of an imperial city?" That was a fair question in the 1820s, for in the next several decades the nation and its capital faced a challenge which threatened the very existence of the Union.

1830-1870: A Time of Trial

Slowly, silently, 30,000 mourners marched down Pennsylvania Avenue behind the riderless horse and the black, high-canopied hearse, the first of many such processions Washington would witness. The city through which Lincoln's funeral cortege passed in 1865 was far different from the one that existed a half-century before. Gone forever was the small sparsely settled seat of an infant nation. Its place had been taken by the noisy, crowded, and growing capital of a country strong enough to survive four years of civil war. Though the city's population only grew from 19,000 in 1830 to 23,000 in 1840, the next three decades saw a steady increase—to 40,000 in 1850, 61,000 in 1860, and a dramatic rise to 109,000 by 1870.

Continuing improvements in transportation—canals, turnpikes, and railroads—eased the city's isolation, but with progress came problems. One of the city's proudest hopes for commercial growth, the Chesapeake and Ohio Canal, proved an embarrassing and expensive enterprise. Planned in the early 1820s, the canal was intended to link Washington with Pittsburgh. After the

Home of the First Family yet the property of the people, the White House has witnessed many domestic scenes and grand public occasions in its more than 180-year existence.

23

Army Board of Engineers calculated the cost of the complete canal at more than 22 million dollars, a shortened version reaching only to Cumberland, Maryland, was authorized at an estimated 4½ million dollars.

The canal would never be the economic success its boosters hoped for; railroads would soon prove more efficient. In one of history's many telling coincidences, ground-breaking ceremonies on the canal were held on July 4, 1828, the same day a similar ceremony was held in Baltimore for the Baltimore and Ohio Railroad. By September 1831, when the first section of the C&O Canal was opened, the city was substantially in debt, so much so that by the time the B&O Railroad reached the outskirts of the capital in 1835, the city had more than 1½ million dollars in canal debts. Only federal assumption of the debt rescued the city from its financial burden. This particular bit of federal largesse belied the prevailing apathy with which Congress viewed the capital. Most congressmen were mere wayfarers who fled the city's "miasmatic" conditions whenever Congress recessed. Indicative of congressional apathy toward the city, Congress returned Alexandria to Virginia's jurisdiction in 1846 following only limited debate.

The federal presence, whether indifferent or beneficent, was a circumstance peculiar to the capital, but the city shared problems faced by other urban areas. Public works, schools, relief for the poor, and law enforcement all competed for a portion of an overburdened city budget. Sanitation continued to be an ever present problem. The Washington Canal remained a shallow,

Water highway channels barge traffic to Georgetown in the 1800s (left), where the Chesapeake and Ohio Canal, foreground, connects with the Potomac Aqueduct Bridge. Today restored, the C&O Canal adds to the historical flavor of modern Georgetown (above). Barge rides through a pre-Civil War lock (below) recall a bygone era.

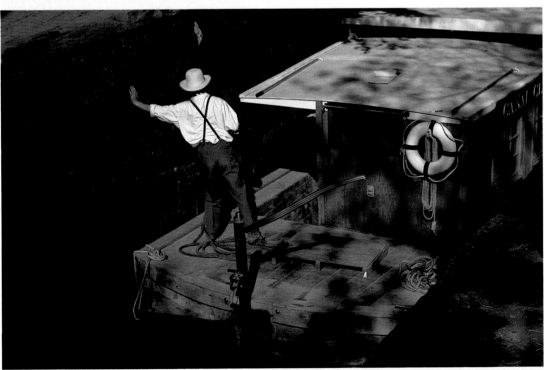

stagnant scar on the Mall, and cisterns and wells still served as the main water supply.

Even an abundant water supply would have been insufficient to deal with the recurring terror of 19th-century cities: fire. Fire-fighting techniques were primitive. Bucket brigades were inefficient and volunteer fire companies were often little more than warring street gangs with colorful names such as "Plug-Uglies." When an arsonist burned the Treasury building to the ground in 1833, even the presence of former President John Quincy Adams in the bucket brigade—according to one Washington legend—could not save the building. Three years later the Post Office burned. Both

were rebuilt, the Treasury as a larger four-story structure at 15th and Pennsylvania.

Buildings ruined by fire could be restored; lives lost in epidemics spawned in the city's filth could not. For several weeks in the summer of 1832, Washington's streets echoed with the cry of "Bring out the dead," as carts collected the victims of an outbreak of Asiatic cholera. Medical treatment—bleeding, and heroic doses of calomel—did more harm than good. Though the epidemic began among German and Irish immigrant workers on the C&O Canal, no class was immune. Marcia Burnes Van Ness, philanthropist and wife of the mayor, died of the disease while nursing the sick.

*U*nion Army troops (left) drill on the Capitol grounds during the Civil War, which filled Washington to brimming with soldiers. Their Commander in Chief, Abraham Lincoln (above), appears haggard but happy: The day before he sat for this photo in 1865, the President had learned of Robert E. Lee's surrender at Appomattox. Abolitionists cheered as the war's close brought an end to slavery throughout the nation. The slave trade had existed even in the capital, as the 1836 broadside below decries.

SLAVE MARKET OF AMERICA.

THE WORD OF GOD.

"ALL THINGS WHATSOEVER YE WOULD THAT MEN SHOULD DO TO YOU, DO YE EVEN SO TO THEM, FOR THIS IS THE LAW AND THE PROPHETS."
"AND THEY SIGHED BY REASON OF THE BONDAGE, AND THEY CRIED, AND THEIR CRY CAME UP UNTO GOD BY REASON OF THE BONDAGE, AND GOD HEARD THEIR GROANING."
US SAITH THE LORD, EXECUTE JUDGMENT IN THE MORNING, AND DELIVER HIM THAT IS SPOILED OUT OF THE HANDS OF THE OPPRESSOR, LEST MY FURY GO OUT LIKE FIRE, AND BURN THAT NONE CAN QUENCH IT, BECAUSE OF THE EVIL OF YOUR DOINGS."

THE DECLARATION OF AMERICAN INDEPENDENCE.

"WE HOLD THESE TRUTHS TO BE SELF-EVIDENT;—THAT ALL MEN ARE CREATED EQUAL; THAT THEY ARE ENDOWED BY THEIR CREATOR WITH CERTAIN UNALIENABLE RIGHTS; THAT AMONG THESE ARE LIFE, LIBERTY, AND THE PURSUIT OF HAPPINESS."

THE CONSITUTION OF THE UNITED STATES.

"THE CITIZENS OF EACH STATE SHALL BE ENTITLED TO ALL THE PRIVILEGES AND IMMUNITIES OF CITIZENS OF THE SEVERAL STATES."—Article 4, Section 2.
"CONGRESS SHALL MAKE NO LAW ABRIDGING THE FREEDOM OF SPEECH OR OF THE PRESS, OR OF THE RIGHT OF THE PEOPLE PEACEABLY TO ASSEMBLE, AND TO PETITION THE GOVERNMENT FOR A REDRESS OF GRIEVANCES."—Amend. I, Amendment.
'GRESS SHALL HAVE POWER TO EXERCISE EXCLUSIVE LEGISLATION, IN ALL CASES WHATSOEVER, OVER SUCH DISTRICT (NOT EXCEEDING TEN MILES SQUARE) AS MAY, BY CESSION OF PARTICULAR STATES AND THE ACCEPTANCE OF CONGRESS, BECOME THE SEAT OF GOVERNMENT OF THE UNITED STATES."—Article 1, Section 8.

CONSTITUTIONS OF THE STATES.

"EVERY CITIZEN MAY FREELY SPEAK, WRITE, AND PUBLISH HIS SENTIMENTS ON ALL SUBJECTS, BEING RESPONSIBLE FOR THE ABUSE OF THAT LIBERTY." *Constitutions of Maine, Connecticut, New-York, Pennsylvania, Delaware, Ohio, Indiana, Illinois, Tennessee, Louisiana, Alabama, Mississippi, and Missouri.*
" THE FREEDOM OF THE PRESS IS ONE OF THE GREAT BULWARKS OF LIBERTY, AND THEREFORE OUGHT NEVER TO BE RESTRAINED."—North Carolina.
"THE LIBERTY OF THE PRESS OUGHT TO BE INVIOLABLY PRESERVED."—Maryland.
"THE FREEDOM OF THE PRESS IS ONE OF THE GREAT BULWARKS OF LIBERTY, AND CAN NEVER BE RESTRAINED DUT BY DESPOTIC GOVERNMENTS."—Virginia. *Other States nearly the same.*

DISTRICT OF COLUMBIA.

| "THE LAND OF THE FREE." | THE RESIDENCE OF 7000 SLAVES. | "THE HOME OF THE OPPRESSED." |

READING OF THE DECLARATION OF INDEPENDENCE.

PART OF WASHINGTON CITY.

CAPITOL OF THE UNITED STATES. "Ham Congress."

RIGHT TO INTERFERE.

Physicians pointed out that the epidemic also was "extremely fatal to our colored population, and more especially to the free blacks." Washington had a sizeable black community prior to the Civil War, averaging from 20 to 30 percent of the city's population. Despite being subjected to restrictions such as curfews and bonds for good behavior, Washington's free blacks established a strong community, with schools and churches, including the African Methodist Episcopal Church formed in 1820.

Many humanitarians found the presence of slavery in the nation's capital a disgrace. Slave gangs marched in chains down the avenues past the Capitol on their way to Alexandria auction lots. One slave pen, an infamous "yellow house on Seventh Street," stood in full view of the Capitol. Antislavery sentiment grew, but fear of slave insurrection remained strong. In 1835 mobs attacked a church, a school, and several tenements in the black community after one of Mrs. William Thornton's slaves, allegedly incited by abolitionist literature, attempted to murder her.

Washington's location made it a center for runaway slaves. In 1848 the schooner *Pearl* was captured on the Potomac with 76 slaves bound for freedom in the North. Even after the slave trade was abolished in the District of Columbia as a provision of the Compromise of 1850, blacks were subjected to harsh treatment. Arrests of blacks were three times as frequent as those of whites; black testimony had no validity against whites; and courts often handed out harsh punishments to blacks for trivial offenses.

On the eve of the Civil War, Washington was a city whose potential was yet to be fulfilled, as symbolized by the Capitol's unfinished dome and by the one-third-completed Washington Monument rising on the Mall. The Capitol's low copper-covered wooden dome, designed by Charles Bulfinch, had been removed so work could begin on a higher cast-iron dome, designed by Thomas U. Walter to complement the new House and Senate wings then under construction. Though work on the Washington Monument, begun in 1848, was temporarily discontinued in 1854 due to lack of funds, other construction continued to change the appearance of the capital.

The red sandstone Smithsonian Castle, the first testament to the legacy of English philanthropist James Smithson, graced the Mall in 1855. The White House had taken on the appearance of a plantation mansion, surrounded by greenhouses, fruit trees, and flower gardens. Opposite Pennsylvania

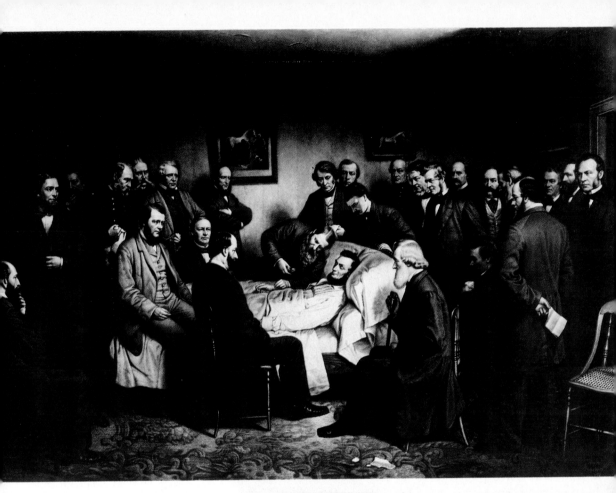

Struck down by a bullet in the head, President Abraham Lincoln lies in the Petersen house (above) across the street from Ford's Theatre (opposite, right). On Good Friday in 1865, Lincoln had gone to the theater to watch the play Our American Cousin. *Suddenly a shot rang out in the President's box. Assassin John Wilkes Booth, brandishing a dagger, caught a boot spur on a draping flag as he leaped from the box (opposite, left). Mortally wounded, Lincoln was carried to the Petersen house. In the front parlor (right)— today restored with furnishings of the period—Mrs. Lincoln kept a night-long vigil. The President died the next morning. One mourner was said to observe: "Now he belongs to the ages."*

29

HERITAGE

Avenue, in Lafayette Square, stood Clark Mills' equestrian statue of Andrew Jackson, his horse dramatically balanced on its hind legs. Though the Mall area was still a malodorous, malarial marsh, an aqueduct begun in 1853 provided fresh water for homes and public fountains by 1859.

Several hotels symbolized the city's gradual maturation. The National, Brown's, the Kirkwood, and above all, the Willard Hotel at 14th and Pennsylvania Avenue, were centers of lobbying and political society. The Willard's cuisine—fried oysters, steak and onions, pâté de foie gras in copious quantities—might have offended European tastes, but Americans found it irresistible.

Outside the federal enclave, the city remained a collection of communities with names such as the Northern Liberties, Negro Hill, English Hill, and Swampoodle.

*H*eart of the world's largest complex of public museums, the sandstone Castle of the Smithsonian Institution lifts towers, turrets, and pinnacles above the Mall. The structure serves as the administrative center for myriad activities that shed enlightenment in the fields of art, history, and the sciences. A half-million dollar bequest by English scientist James Smithson led to the organization's founding in 1846. The Smithsonian's ever-growing collection of Americana has earned the institution the affectionate nickname of the Nation's Attic.

Lawlessness was rampant in many poverty-stricken areas of the city. An 1858 Senate report commented: "Riot and bloodshed are of daily occurrence. Innocent and unoffending persons are shot, stabbed, and otherwise shamefully maltreated, and not unfrequently the offender is not even arrested."

Even had Washington's citizens been more peaceable, the police force was inadequate to maintain order. The city had a total of only 57 regular police officers in 1851, while Baltimore, with a smaller area to patrol, had a force of 400. Crime, whatever the size of the police force, was not confined to the poor. Congressmen brawled on the House floor, Preston Brooks savagely assaulted Senator Charles Sumner in the Senate Chamber, and Congressman Daniel Sickles murdered his wife's lover in Lafayette Square on a Sunday afternoon in 1859.

Violence in the nation's capital during the 1850s was but a portent of the coming Civil War. When war followed Lincoln's election, the capital was transformed into a huge army camp ringed with forts. From 1861 to 1865 soldiers filled nearly every available space in the city, from the Capitol Rotunda to the Georgetown College campus. The war came uncomfortably close to Washington in the summer of 1864 when Confederate forces under Gen. Jubal Early executed a lightning raid through Maryland to the very outskirts of the city.

Living and dying reminders of the war were always present in the city's hospitals, crowded with as many as 50,000 suffering men. Courageous nurses led by Clara Barton tended the wounded. Tarnished angels of mercy also ministered to soldiers: Prostitution flourished as police authorities took a lenient attitude. One whole section of the city's Second Ward was renamed Hooker's Division. Decent citizens were outraged—one brothel adjoined the First Baptist Church—but periodic raids did little to discourage the practice, though they did succeed in removing its more offensive aspects from public view.

Order was maintained and the capital functioned well throughout the war. Work

Abandoned stump of the Washington Monument (left, at top) looms above Potomac River marshes near formal gardens of the Department of Agriculture in 1875. The failure of a national funds appeal (below) in 1854— along with the effects of theft, politics, and the Civil War—halted work on the marble obelisk for more than two decades. The 3,300-pound marble capstone (above) finally topped the completed monument in 1884.

APPEAL TO THE COUNTRY
IN BEHALF OF THE

WASHINGTON

NATIONAL MONUMENT.

FELLOW-CITIZENS:

The Monument so nobly undertaken by a few of our patriotic countrymen, to commemorate the worth and services of the Father of the Country, having reached 154 feet, of the 517, according to its plan, at a cost of about $230,000, needs your prompt and zealous support to raise funds, now nearly exhausted, to carry it on after the present month of June. Unless contributions are made this great National Work must be discontinued, if the Board of Managers, who render their services gratuitous, do not incur a debt upon their own responsibility. Is their patriotism to be so taxed, or shall this work begun in patriotism be a monument of national disgrace? Surely there are a sufficient number of noble hearted patriots in the land to prevent this.

Nothing but a small contribution from all, in proportion to their means, if only from a dime to a dollar each, is wanted for the completion of the Monument. The question is asked, will not such a contribution be made by every one? Will the people of this great country leave to a few the honor, after long years of trial and toil, of erecting a Monument worthy of the great and good Washington; or shall it be a National Monument from the whole people? That the Monument should stop short of one third of the plan proposed, no patriotic citizen can believe!

But the time for making contributions can be no longer delayed. Let every citizen ask himself Have I discharged my obligation towards the Father of my Country: have I contributed my share to the Monument to be raised in his honor? If not, let him at once make his contribution, however small. Let it be made singly or by associations. But be sure it be made. Delay is hazardous to the great undertaking. The payment can be made to your Postmaster, or whoever may be most convenient to you, so that the duty of an American citizen be discharged. Every patriotic citizen surely will aid in forwarding the money received for the advancement of the great work. Will he not render that aid now? The Board of Managers confidently trust that this appeal will not be made in vain.

OFFICERS:

FRANKLIN PIERCE, *President of the United States, and ex-officio President.*
ARCH. HENDERSON, *First Vice President.*
JOHN T. TOWERS, *Mayor of Washington, and ex-officio Second Vice President.*
THOS. CARBERRY, *Third Vice President.*
J. B. H. SMITH, *Treasurer.*
JOHN CARROLL BRENT, *Secretary.*

MANAGERS:

WINFIELD SCOTT,	JOHN W. MAURY,
N. TOWSON,	WALTER JONES,
PETER FORCE,	THOS. BLAGDEN,
W. W. SEATON,	WALTER LENOX,
W. A. BRADLEY,	M. F. MAURY,
W. W. CORCORAN,	T. HARTLEY CRAWFORD,
P. R. FENDALL,	BENJ. OGLE TAYLOE.
ELISHA WHITTLESEY.	

continued on the Capitol dome. "If people see the Capitol going on," President Lincoln affirmed, "it is a sign we intend the Union shall go on." On December 2, 1863, the dome was crowned with Thomas Crawford's 19½-foot Statue of Freedom, a bronze figure of a woman in flowing garments resting her left hand on a shield and her right hand on a sheathed sword.

But "the fateful lightning" of the Union's "terrible swift sword" would not be sheathed for another 16 months. At the cost of more than 600,000 lives the Union was preserved and Washington was once more the capital of all the United States. Thousands of former slaves swelled the city's streets, many no doubt hoping for a glimpse of the Great Emancipator. Yet the war was to exact one final casualty, the man whose words offered hope to so many: "With malice toward none, with charity for all, . . . let us strive to finish the work we are in, to bind up the nation's wounds . . . to do all which may achieve and cherish a just and lasting peace." For the country, the end of the war

meant the loss of a great national leader. For Washington, it marked the beginning of an era of peace and the pursuit of prosperity.

1870-1930: Prosperity and Growth

"For reasons which many persons thought ridiculous, Mrs. Lightfoot Lee decided to pass the winter in Washington." So began Henry Adams' anonymously published 1880 novel, *Democracy*, a tale of graft and corruption in the Washington of the 1870s. The merely curious, such as Adams' heroine, were not the only ones enticed by the power of the federal government. Now the capital of a nation embarking on a period of rapid economic growth, Washington attracted both the great and the greedy. Often, as Mrs. Lightfoot Lee discovered, it would be impossible to separate the two.

After a brief experiment in reconstruction, Congress was quite willing to rid itself of the city's problems. In 1871 Congress granted the District of Columbia territorial status, though it was clear there was no

*A*bolitionist editor Frederick Douglass *(above, right) spoke out eloquently for black equality and women's rights in post-Civil War Washington, where a mushrooming population forced many unskilled blacks to live in squalid alley dwellings (opposite). Active religious organizations, such as the congregation below, helped mold a strong black community in Washington in the face of segregation. The A Street home of the one-time slave Douglass (above) today houses the Museum of African Art, whose permanent collection includes more than 8,000 objects.*

35

intention that statehood would follow. The territorial form of government consisted of a presidentially appointed governor, council, Board of Public Works, and Board of Public Health; a popularly elected house of delegates; and a nonvoting delegate to Congress. All of President Grant's nominees were Republicans, and three of the 11 men nominated to the council were black, including former slave Frederick Douglass, then a lecturer and newspaper editor.

In its three years of existence, the territorial government achieved much that was good and necessary. The Board of Health, led by John Mercer Langston, instituted new regulations designed to curb the city's "prolific generators of plague and pestilence." Stray animals were impounded—ironically the first were three of President Grant's own horses—389 unsanitary buildings were condemned, accurate vital statistics were compiled, and efforts were undertaken to educate the public on hygiene. Though unsanitary tenement dwellings were condemned, even federal office buildings were found to be unhealthful. According to the

Alexander R. Shepherd (above), the man who "ran" Washington in the early 1870s, improved the city by paving streets and building sidewalks (below)—and grew rich in the process. In the 1880s and '90s the city flowered with Gilded Age elegance, reflected in the ornate dining room of the Christian Heurich mansion (opposite).

board's report on the Treasury, "... rooms are crowded with clerks and employees much beyond their capacity. These, for an average of six hours per day, breathe an atmosphere saturated with carbonic acid."

While the Board of Health quietly won praise for its work, the real force in the new government, the Board of Public Works, managed major municipal improvements. It also destroyed the territorial government and brought bankruptcy and shame to the city. Dominated by one man, Alexander R. Shepherd, the board oversaw the creation of 120 miles of sewers, 150 miles of road improvements, 208 miles of sidewalks, 30 miles of water mains, 39 miles of gas lines, 3½ million cubic yards of excavation, and the planting of more than 60,000 trees.

As the city neared the 20th century, few of Washington's leaders seemed aware of the existence of a "secret city." Hidden from sight, yet within walking distance of the capital's monuments and mansions, was another Washington. In alleys throughout the city, thousands of the poor lived in ramshackle shanties or overcrowded, unventilated tenements. An 1897 survey placed the total alley population at 17,244, of which

Carrying the colors down Pennsylvania Avenue, President Woodrow Wilson (above, center foreground) leads a parade welcoming victorious soldiers home from the battlefields of France in February 1919. On January 8, 1919, the President had delivered his most important speech, "The Fourteen Points," a framework for world peace. The Great War officially ended in June 1919. Nearly three months later, in a victory parade led by Gen. John Pershing (left), troops marched past the Treasury Annex under a specially built Arch of Triumph that spanned Pennsylvania Avenue.

43

*T*urn of the century vista on Pennsylvania Avenue: Visitors in the south plaza of the Treasury building, foreground, enjoy a popular view of the Capitol. Today a rush of motor vehicles has replaced the electric streetcars and horse-drawn carriages. Some historic landmarks, however, still stand along the avenue, such as the cathedral-towered Post Office, in the distance at right, and the Willard Hotel, behind the tall tree at left. Begun in 1836, the Treasury building blocked the uninterrupted line from the White House to the Capitol, disrupting part of L'Enfant's design.

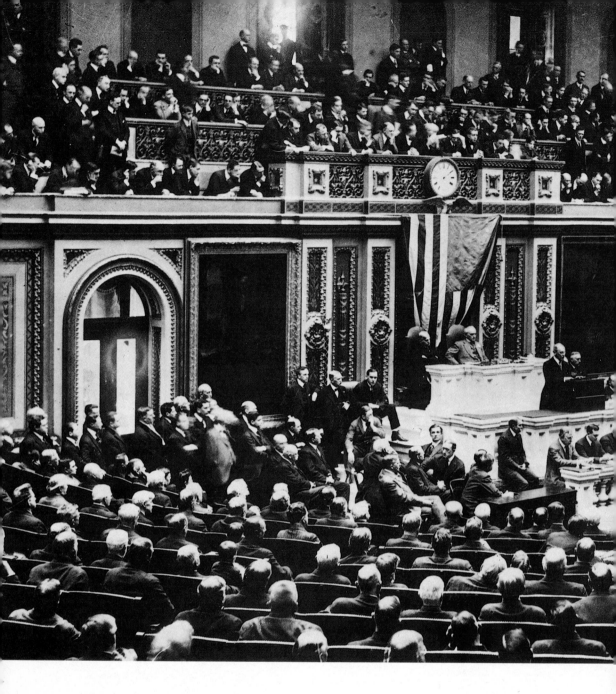

"Boss" Shepherd epitomized the uncompromising—some would say unprincipled—business ethic of the age. Authorized to spend only four million dollars on public works, Shepherd dispensed more than 20 million in three years. Though no one has been able to determine the extent of graft, it was obvious Shepherd benefited from his position. His blunt manner angered many Washingtonians. When the B&O Railroad delayed removal of its tracks from the west side of the Capitol grounds, Shepherd dispatched 300 workmen at night to tear them up, bury the rail bed, and deposit the tracks at the train station. If anyone objected to such tactics, Shepherd said they could "git up and git."

Eventually Shepherd was the one who had to go, to a self-imposed exile in Mexico, where he became a silver magnate. The territorial form of government went too, replaced by three presidentially appointed commissioners, ending this brief experiment in limited self-government. Shepherd's departure signaled the beginning of

an orgy of real estate speculation lasting until the 1890s. Property values climbed, real estate firms multiplied, and more than 2,400 buildings were constructed in 1887 alone. Opulent Victorian mansions marked the taste of Washington's social elite. Two excellent examples, Curtis J. Hillyer's residence and the Christian Heurich mansion, epitomized the ostentation of the rich.

As real estate values skyrocketed, average Washingtonians found affordable housing scarce. "It is strange," one critic noted, "that the capitalists and moneyed men of Washington seeking good opportunities for investment never think of building... within the reach of poor men and government clerks," a particularly astute observation since the number of government clerks was rising—from 7,800 in 1880 to 23,000 in 1890—creating added demand for housing and public services.

Fortunately, the period's prosperity appeared to "trickle down" to the average citizen. Government remained the major employer and public works provided thousands

Addressing a joint session of Congress, President Woodrow Wilson cuts diplomatic ties with Germany in February 1917 (left). Less than two months later the U.S. entered World War I. Wartime Washington boomed with an influx of people and a surge of new building, such as the construction of war workers' dormitories in Union Station Plaza (below). By 1918 The Great War had changed the capital from a leisurely town into a bustling metropolis.

of jobs for common laborers on projects such as the National Museum, the Washington Monument, the new Post Office, and the Library of Congress building. The depression of 1893, though mild in Washington, was brought home in the spring of 1894 when hundreds of unemployed men led by "General" Coxey of Ohio descended upon the Capitol to demand federal relief measures.

Depression and unemployment were far from many Washingtonians' minds in the closing decade of the 19th century. With prosperity came the leisure time to enjoy the city and the wealth to improve it. Congress had considered acquiring the upper Rock Creek valley for a park since the 1860s, but not until the 1890s was money appropriated to create Rock Creek Park, "a pleasuring ground for the . . . people of the United States," soon followed by creation of the National Zoo and Potomac Park. Some municipal improvements detracted from the city's appearance. Since 1845 West-

ern Union had planted its "uncouth poles at will in front of any man's premises without his consent." After 1878 the telephone company added its poles and wires, and in the 1890s horse-drawn streetcars gave way to electric trolleys. Washington, "a city of trees," was in danger of becoming a city of poles and electric wire. The city commissioners were able to meet this problem by requiring most wires to be laid underground.

Though the City Commission still managed municipal affairs, citizens were able to voice their opinions through civic associations and the Board of Trade, founded in 1889. Numbering Washington's foremost businessmen and professionals among its members, the Board of Trade soon became powerful. Within two years Congress and the city commissioners were consulting the board for advice, and, according to historian Constance McLaughlin Green, "by the end of the century it was an open secret that the commissioners themselves owed their office to the board's directors."

more than 16,000 were black. Centers of crime, disease, and death, alley dwellings were a festering reproach to the complacent prosperity of the period.

By and large, Washington's white citizens believed charity should be extended only to the "worthy" poor, and most blacks were not found worthy: "... alley evils are simply due to the racial traits of their principal inhabitants—the colored people," wrote one Washingtonian representing the prevailing white attitude. In reality a rigid color barrier confined most of Washington's black citizens to menial positions and lives of poverty. Unable to break through the color barrier into white society, blacks were forced to create their own separate community.

The constraints of segregation split the black community along distinct class lines. An upper class, mainly descended from Washington's leading antebellum free black families, formed a small black aristocracy. The middle class was composed of black government employees, businessmen, and tradesmen. The lower, most-populous class, was made up of recent arrivals from the South, living from hand to mouth. To maintain their own worth vis-à-vis the white community, many upper-class blacks took pains to dissociate themselves from the rank and file, behavior some saw as counterproductive. For the city at large, segregation meant that thousands of black men and women were not allowed to contribute their full abilities to the city's growth.

In the first decades of the 20th century, official Washington pursued plans to beautify the city. The catalyst was the Park Commission, created through the efforts of Senator James McMillan in 1901. The commission's general plan recommended congressional and judicial office buildings to face the Capitol, museums and public galleries to line the Mall, and a memorial to Abraham Lincoln at the far end of the Mall, along with gardens, fountains, and a reflecting pool. The railroad tracks that still crossed

the Mall were to be torn out and a grand Union Station constructed a few blocks north of the Capitol.

Professional jealousies and petty bureaucratic squabblings prevented full implementation of the McMillan Commission report. However, as Glenn Brown of the American Institute of Architects attested, the plan came to exercise "great moral force." That moral force broadened to include social reform. Concerned that city planners were expressing only "a superficial quest for beauty," some Washingtonians sought to provide decent living conditions and broader economic opportunities for the poor.

Infused with the progressive spirit of the first decades of the 20th century and the realization that environmental factors played an important role in poverty and crime, reformers worked through organizations such as the Associated Charities to agitate for legislation to remove the grossest evils of alley dwelling. Congress passed an alley dwelling act in 1914, largely due to the efforts of First Lady Ellen Wilson. The act had no real power, but the numbers of alley dwellers did decline.

Washington's progressive spirit became a casualty to the changes brought by the First World War, which altered forever the city's size, appearance, and composition. As thousands flocked to the capital to perform war work, the city's population rose 32 percent in a decade, from 330,000 in 1910 to more than 437,000 by 1920. Even with every available house crammed with new arrivals, there was not enough housing. Temporary office buildings were thrown up on the Mall and dormitories were built between the Capitol and Union Station. Much to the dismay of the city's older residents, many of the new arrivals remained after the war, living in impersonal apartment houses. Washingtonians felt a sense of loss, a feeling that the intimacy of the prewar city was gone, replaced

Jobless veterans lobby at the Capitol in July 1932. Thousands of marchers, known as the Bonus Army, pressured Congress for immediate payment of a not-yet-due bonus for World War I soldiers. Federal troops eventually evicted the luckless veterans from their encampments.

by the impersonality of the modern world.

During the 1920s, Washington's population grew to 487,000, and the city began to take on a cosmopolitan air. Tourism increased, the Lincoln Memorial was dedicated in 1922, and the first Cherry Blossom Festival was held in 1927. The National Park and Planning Commission was created to coordinate city growth, and the Fine Arts Commission began work on the Federal Triangle. From gaudy burlesque houses to chamber music concerts in the Library of Congress, the arts flourished during the Roaring Twenties. The Jazz Age infected Washington too; a young musician called Duke Ellington got his start here. There were also reminders of the more serious side of life, such as the 1925 gathering of 25,000 members of the Ku Klux Klan on the Washington Monument grounds. But for most Americans, and most Washingtonians, the

Grave but confident leader, President-elect Franklin D. Roosevelt (right) takes the oath of office in March 1933. At far right, beside FDR's son James, stands a solemn Herbert Hoover, the man often blamed for the Great Depression. In the early 1930s destitute Americans nationwide, like those below at Central Union Mission in Washington, lined up for food handouts. FDR's inaugural address lifted the nation's flagging spirits with the reassurance that "the only thing we have to fear is fear itself...."

'20s were a time of carefree self-indulgence.

The automobile, the supreme symbol of the '20s, now commanded L'Enfant's broad avenues and threatened to turn the Mall into a vast parking lot. By 1930 more than 173,000 cars were registered in the city. In spite of a 22-mile-per-hour speed limit, there were 9,400 accidents in 1925 alone. Even the formal procession of the casket of the Unknown Soldier from the Capitol to Arlington Cemetery in 1921 was delayed more than two hours by a traffic jam, and some dignitaries did not reach the cemetery at all.

Few in Washington sensed any signs of trouble in the '20s. The scandals of the Harding Administration were minor irritants—official greed was after all something with which Washingtonians were familiar —and skyrocketing stock market speculation seemed just another sign of good times. As the decade drew to a close, the White House was occupied by Herbert Hoover, a man who had campaigned on the belief that, "We in America today are nearer to the final triumph over poverty than ever before in the history of any land." The stock market crash in 1929 did not appear to have an immediate impact on Washington, but when it did, the course of the city and the entire nation was irrevocably altered.

*S*teel beams replace weak wooden timbers in the White House (above, left). In 1948 a trembling chandelier warned President Harry Truman that the venerable mansion's supports were shaky. Congress ordered a complete renovation, and the Trumans moved into Blair House. Near the project's end, workmen return the Red Room to its former elegance (above). In March 1952 President and Mrs. Truman moved back into the White House (below), whose South Portico featured a second-story balcony designed by the President himself (left).

1930-1980: Challenges and Change

Washington's first exposure to the impact of the Great Depression came in the form of an unusual mass lobbying effort. Though some called them Bolsheviks and traitors, others realized the thousands of veterans who marched on Washington in 1932 were simply victims of the Depression. Remarkably orderly, the "Bonus Army," composed of as many as 20,000 unemployed World War I veterans, sought immediate payment of a bonus not due until 1945. Bivouacked in empty buildings, sheds, warehouses, and a ramshackle camp near a dump in Anacostia, the veterans were assisted by Police Superintendent Pelham D. Glassford, a sympathetic public official who traveled about the city on a big blue motorcycle.

Even after the Bonus Bill died, many veterans vowed to remain in the capital until the bonus was granted. Nearly destitute, the Bonus Army camped on the Anacostia mud flats throughout the summer of '32. President Hoover, refusing to see the veterans, thought the situation was a purely local matter. It did not remain so for long. Late in July trouble broke out when the city police were ordered to evict some squatters from federal buildings on Pennsylvania Avenue. Army troops were called in from nearby Fort Myer. Commanded by Gen. Douglas MacArthur, an immaculate cavalry and tank formation paraded down the avenue.

Suddenly, tear gas bombs exploded and the cavalry charged, putting the astounded veterans to flight. The tanks, commanded by Maj. Dwight D. Eisenhower, blocked the Anacostia bridge while MacArthur's troops moved on to burn out the Bonus Army's main camp. Although MacArthur persisted in the contention that he had saved the nation from imminent revolution, most citizens disagreed, condemning the senseless brutality with which the eviction had been handled. Meanwhile, the full force of the Depression hit the capital, bringing salary cuts, furloughs, reductions in force, and a gloomy outlook.

The city's somber mood did not begin to lift until after Franklin D. Roosevelt's New Deal instilled a spirit of self-confidence.

Scores of new government agencies were staffed by bright young men and women, filled with enthusiasm, although as one later recalled, "we didn't know exactly for what." To critics the burgeoning governmental apparatus, with agencies such as the NRA, AAA, and CCC, seemed reckless and haphazard, like "college professors playing anagrams with alphabet soup." But it did create jobs, increasing the federal establishment in Washington from 63,000 in 1933 to more than 93,000 before 1935.

New Deal enthusiasm inspired a construction boom in the '30s, as if the sheer intensity of effort alone could lift the nation out of depression. The Federal Triangle, the Supreme Court Building, the Longworth House Office Building, and the Library of Congress Annex were all constructed or completed in the '30s, and ground was broken for the Jefferson Memorial in 1939. Moreover, nearly 1,800 new apartment buildings, more than 2,300 separate or row houses, and 800 office buildings went up before 1940, all of which prompted one writer to boast of "Washington, The Blest."

During World War II, the city's streets, offices, homes, and apartments again swelled with thousands of servicemen and women and war workers. Though jukeboxes jumped with the tunes of Glenn Miller, Benny Goodman, and the Andrews Sisters, the prevailing atmosphere was one of serious dedication to winning the war.

Since World War II, Washington has become the bustling capital of a world power. Every major national development in the past three decades has had an impact upon the city. The civil rights movement of the late '50s and '60s, the antiwar protests of the '60s and early '70s, and the movement for urban renewal have all affected Washington's development. Today the city is in a state of transition. Granted a form of home rule with an elected mayor and city council under the D.C. Self-Government and Governmental Reorganization Act of 1973, Washington is experiencing a political rebirth.

From a peak of over 800,000 in 1950, the city's population fell to 638,000 by 1980. As the city lost population, the suburbs gained, creating the traffic problems most Washingtonians take for granted. In recent years the trend appears to be reversing, with young couples moving back into the city to restore dilapidated old row houses. The overall appearance of the city is undergoing a similar revitalization. Modern buildings are replacing vacant or run-down structures.

The challenge for Washington today is how best to preserve the heritage of the past while meeting the needs of the present and planning for the future. Although Pierre L'Enfant hoped the federal district would be spacious enough to meet all future needs, the city has already felt its limitations. In the rush to redevelop, many historic structures have been lost or are in danger of being demolished. Given the city's physical limits, many federal agencies have chosen to locate outside the District—led by the Pentagon, and followed by others including the CIA, the National Bureau of Standards, and the National Institutes of Health.

Behind warm smiles of majorettes, a band passes the reviewing stand of President Jimmy Carter in the January cold of Inauguration Day 1977. On the freezing inaugural morning of 1913, President-elect Woodrow Wilson rides with outgoing President William Howard Taft (opposite). An impromptu procession of Navy Yard workers cheering Thomas Jefferson launched the Inaugural Parade tradition in 1805.

Meanwhile, new construction in the city has included the Rayburn House Office Building, the Hoover FBI building, the James Madison building of the Library of Congress, and the Hart Senate Office Building. The city continues to inspire grand visions: The recently completed Master Plan for the United States Capitol, charting growth for the next 50 to 75 years, identifies potential sites for new congressional office buildings and also provides for the closing of selected streets to traffic, extensive landscaping, and the construction of underground parking.

Although much remains to be done to make Washington the model city it should be, the contrast between the city today and that of just a century ago could not be greater. The Mall area, the Capitol, the White House, and the monuments—the areas tourists most wish to see—reflect the foresight of the city's founders. But Washington has become more than a collection of marble monuments to the past; it has become a dynamic city with a character and a charm all its own.

FOLLOWING PAGES: *Heart of the capital winks with lights at day's end. The city's broad avenues, stately buildings, and sweeping parks bear witness to L'Enfant's grand design.*

51

Washington Present:
Our Nation's Capital Today

By Richard Striner

Washington today is a city of extraordinary changes and extraordinary continuities. The federal government accounts for much of the city's character. But though the capital is stamped with the past, it is also immersed in trends. Indeed, the classical buildings and the timeless monuments survive in an ever-shifting metropolis. Washington's rate of growth is among the most explosive in the nation.

Visitors to Washington frequently remark upon the city's many faces. From a thriving downtown commercial district to an 18th-century port now filled with boutiques and homes for the affluent — from an inner-city core of row houses to a park of woods, paths, and glades extending for miles — our nation's capital displays an everchanging look and feel. The city reveals an overall spirit that compares at its best to Paris. The arcadian vision dreamt in the 18th century lives in Washington today — along with traffic snarls and the frenzy of public affairs.

Capitol Hill is an excellent point from which to overlook the city. Standing on the Capitol's West Front terrace, one is struck by the expansive sweep of the Mall. The Capitol grounds give way to a reflecting pool over which the sculpted figure of Gen. Ulysses S. Grant sits watch and gulls swoop and dive. Farther west are the galleries and museums, along with the towering Washington Monument, the inspiring memorial to Lincoln, and the wooded ridge of Virginia beyond the Potomac. Known as Jenkins' Hill in the colonial era, Capitol Hill today is a focal point for the country, the scene where our elected representatives convene to do the people's work.

The Many Houses of Government

With the floodlights on at night, the Capitol Building is a glowing vision. By day, it is the dominant sight on the Mall. Probably few Washington visitors know that its famous dome is considered a masterpiece of 19th-century engineering. An evolving edifice, the Capitol has expanded much further than was ever imagined by William Thornton, its original designer, whose simple and gracefully proportioned plan in the 1790s received the approval of the city's founders. Expanded wings for the House and Senate and two successive domes, along with an extension of the East Front in the late 1950s, have all but hidden the original sandstone structure under sheaths of marble.

Within, the Capitol comprises a series of grand chambers connected by a maze of passageways and corridors. The central Rotunda, below the dome, contains huge historical paintings by the early American artist John Trumbull and other painters.

Landmark of liberty crowns Capitol Hill in Washington, D.C. Inside the imposing edifice, Congress decides the policies that help govern a nation. The Capitol's gleaming dome echoes those of Old World structures—St. Peter's Basilica in Rome and St. Paul's Cathedral in London.

Here American heroes have lain in flag-draped coffins: the unknown soldiers and the martyred leaders Lincoln, Garfield, McKinley, and Kennedy. Below the Rotunda, in the area known as the Crypt, there was to be a monument to George Washington covering a tomb for the first President. However, Washington's heirs disagreed with the plan, and the bodies of President and Mrs. Washington remained interred at Mount Vernon.

Spread throughout the Capitol Building is the Statuary Hall collection—statues of eminent Americans. The collection was started by an act of Congress in 1864, and every state has been invited to contribute statues of two individuals. From Jefferson Davis and Daniel Webster to Will Rogers and Huey Long, the sculpted figures adorn the Capitol hallways. Among the newest statues are figures of the late Senator Ernest Gruening of Alaska and Mother Joseph, a pioneering nun who was important to the early settlement of Washington State.

The Senate corridors contain the elaborate murals of Constantino Brumidi, an Italian painter and muralist who fled persecution in Italy in 1852. From 1855 until 1880, when he died, Brumidi painted throughout the Capitol. His masterwork is the decoration of the dome, a huge allegorical painting called the "Apotheosis," or glorification, of George Washington. Brumidi's death at 72 came a few months after an accident high in

*P*riceless artwork graces the Capitol: In the Rotunda, a statue of Ulysses S. Grant (right) stands near a canvas showing the victory of American patriots at Saratoga, New York, in 1777. Below, visitors learn about the Rotunda's eight large oil paintings, whose scenes include events from the lives of Columbus, Pocahontas, and the Pilgrims.

the Rotunda, where he had been working on its huge circular frieze.

Though Brumidi's work was continued by Filippo Costaggini, it remained for American muralist Allyn Cox to complete the Rotunda frieze in 1953. Cox went on to create an artistic triumph of his own in a project sponsored by the U.S. Capitol Historical Society and the Daughters of the American Revolution: two series of murals in the House corridors, "Capitol Hall" and "Great Experiment Hall." The first depicts historical events and shows the various meeting places of Congress. The second traces the history of the emerging republic, from the Mayflower Compact to woman suffrage.

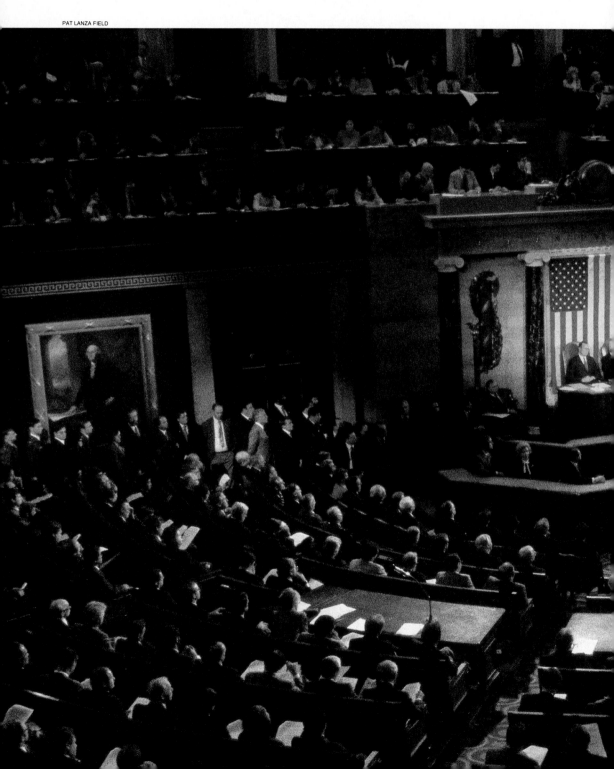

*S*enate and House gather in joint session in the House Chamber (below) to hear President Ronald Reagan (left) deliver his annual State of the Union address. Vice President George Bush—the President of the Senate—and Speaker of the House Thomas P. (Tip) O'Neill, Jr., share the dais behind Mr. Reagan.

Through the halls of the Capitol move the humble and mighty: senators and representatives, pages and congressional staff, tourists and guides, and witnesses at the never-ending hearings. While the Capitol police are among the most diligent guardians of public spaces in the city, they work with the clear understanding that the governed must be allowed to exhort their leaders in person. Strict regulations governing visitors are enforced in the Senate and House chambers, but the offices of senators and congressmen are frequently visited by constituents and lobbyists.

Congressional offices are spread throughout six imposing structures beyond the Capitol Building itself. At the turn of the century, the two houses of Congress were sufficiently large to warrant a separate office building for each. Today, the House of Representatives and the Senate have three office buildings apiece. The buildings for the House are named for Speakers Joseph Cannon, Nicholas Longworth, and Sam Rayburn. The Senate office buildings are named for Senators Richard Russell, Everett McKinley Dirksen, and Philip Hart. The Senate's buildings are located directly northeast of the Capitol, and the office buildings of the House are immediately south. Subways connect all of the buildings to the Capitol, enabling congressmen to quickly reach the floor of the House or Senate.

The Capitol grounds are a tribute to an artist who worked with nature—Frederick Law Olmsted, the preeminent American 19th-century landscape architect. From his triumph in New York City, the designing of Central Park, Olmsted came to Washington in 1874 to accept the challenge of refining the Capitol grounds. Olmsted's touch lives at almost every point around the Capitol. Not only were the Capitol grounds designed under his direction, but the elegant West Front terraces also were added to the Capitol

Building, along with a lovely grotto on the Senate side of the Capitol grounds, where a bubbling spring is contained within a sheltered, rocky enclosure.

Close by is the Botanic Garden, which traces its beginnings to the early 19th century. The garden's first greenhouse was constructed by the government in 1842 to house a collection from the South Seas. This greenhouse was located at 8th and F Streets, N.W. The first official U.S. Botanic Garden was located on the Mall in 1850, and the present conservatory was completed in 1933. Along with the collections displayed throughout the year in the garden, a variety of seasonal shows are presented, such as Christmas displays, chrysanthemum shows, and extensive floral displays in the spring.

To the east of the Capitol stands the Library of Congress. Founded in 1800 as a reference source for Congress, the library suffered two disastrous fires in the 19th century. In 1897 the library was moved from the Capitol Building to a newly completed Italian Renaissance-style structure. The lavish ornamental detail, both within the building and in its exterior, is striking. The library features delicately crafted mosaics and numerous murals. Behind the main library building is an annex completed in 1939. Reflecting the architectural style known as Art Deco, the building was originally named for Thomas Jefferson. It was renamed for John Adams in 1980, though it still has a Jefferson Reading Room.

The newest addition to the library complex is the building on Independence Avenue named for James Madison. Together, these buildings make up the central domain of the library, which some believe to be the largest single repository of knowledge anywhere in the world. The library's holdings, representing more than 450 different languages, today amount to nearly 80 million

Palatial opulence distinguishes the Main Reading Room of the Library of Congress. Sea shells, griffins, cherubs, and garlands embellish the chamber's magnificent dome. Between the marble columns, galleries lead to 44,000 volumes contained in alcoves around the room, a small portion of the library's huge collection. Founded in 1800, the Library of Congress continues its main role of providing research and reference information to members of the House and the Senate.

Delicate hybrid, Laeliocattleya canhamiana *numbers among the 200 orchid plants displayed daily at the U.S. Botanic Garden, near the Capitol. A jungle of exotic plants basks beneath the glass shell of the garden's conservatory (opposite) and includes tropical, subtropical, and desert plants from around the world. Outside, in a one-acre park, begonias bloom in a riot of color.*

CYNTHIA B. SCUDDER

books, pamphlets, newspapers, manuscripts, microfilms, motion pictures, still photographs, recordings, maps, posters, and relics. Among its treasures are a Gutenberg Bible, a draft of the Declaration of Independence in Jefferson's handwriting (the final version rests in the National Archives), and even the contents of Abraham Lincoln's pockets on the night of his murder.

The Library of Congress is a scholarly research institution on the order of nothing else in the country. In its 19 reading rooms, researchers can immerse themselves in arcane linguistic or mathematical studies, read 19th-century popular magazines or political journals, or listen to medieval music or to a recording of James Joyce reciting passages from *Finnegans Wake*. Anyone over high-school age may use the library, but priority service is given to congressmen and their staffs. A special division, the Congressional Research Service, is equipped to respond to any congressional query. The volume of such requests currently exceeds 400,000 a year. In addition, the law library is available to congressmen and their staffs, as well as to the public. Such is the invaluable center of learning only minutes away from the Capitol.

A second of the three coequal branches of the federal government is represented on Capitol Hill: the Supreme Court. For years the Court was beholden in a way to the legislative branch, since it met within the Capitol Building. Not until 1935 did the Court have a building of its own, a neoclassical-style structure in which, as one anonymous Supreme Court Justice is reputed to have remarked, the members of the Court would appear as so many "black beetles in the temple of Karnak." Designed by architect Cass Gilbert and approved by Chief Justice William Howard Taft, the building reflects a dignified grandeur: 24,700 pieces of marble were required just for the exterior walls.

Within the Supreme Court building are the chambers in which our highest judicial officers tend to the business of the nation's 13 federal circuits. Each Justice has jurisdiction over one or more of the circuits. In their collective role, the Justices serve as the land's highest court of appeal. They also exercise judicial review of legislation when a case is brought before them, a function pioneered by John Marshall in the landmark decision of *Marbury v. Madison.*

By tradition, the Supreme Court Justices fulfill their roles with an air of detachment unusual in Washington. Though the Court always sits in open session, much of its work is cloaked in secrecy, a confidentiality pierced on rare occasions, such as through an interview or memoir. The Justices work in richly appointed three-room suites. About 300 persons are employed by the Court to see to its orderly functioning, and especially to the production and printing of judicial decisions. A number of historical exhibits grace the building, and citizens enter with a feeling of walking into a shrine.

The focal point for the third branch of government, the executive, sits along Pennsylvania Avenue to the west of Capitol Hill. The simplicity and beauty of James Hoban's original design for the White House has survived a number of proposed expansions. Although the residential and office functions of the White House were separated in 1902 through the addition of a low Executive Wing, the central portion of the building retains the understated beauty of the 18th-century country houses that inspired its architect.

Almost every President has changed the decor of the Executive Mansion to suit his taste—and that of his First Lady. From 1948 to 1952, the building was virtually stripped to a bare shell for the installation of structural steel and other repairs. In the renovation, the paneling and interior details were carefully numbered, stored, and later replaced.

Despite all the changes in the White House over the years, there are obvious continuities, and even the changes add up to a kind of tradition: One looks for the traces of particular Presidents. As you pass through the North Portico or pause in any portion of a White House tour to take in the surroundings, you are struck by a sense of the personalities that once were so vivid here: Johnson, Kennedy, Eisenhower, Truman, and FDR; the dour Coolidge and the prim Wilson—one sees reminders all the way

Graceful South Portico of the White House, the oldest public building in Washington, overlooks the President's Park, a tree-dotted lawn with fountains and flower beds. The Executive Mansion has served as the home of U.S. Presidents since 1800, the year John and Abigail Adams, its first residents, moved in.

HERITAGE

In the White House Oval Office, Senator Howard H. Baker, Jr. (above, left), Representative Silvio O. Conte (center), and Senator Mark O. Hatfield watch as President Reagan signs an appropriations resolution into law. The President's desk (opposite) was carved from oak timbers from the British ship Resolute *and given to President Rutherford B. Hayes by Queen Victoria.*

back to Thomas Jefferson and John Adams.

The oldest public building in Washington, the White House sits amid 18 acres of greenery. A high wrought-iron fence surrounds the mansion, along which lines of tourists assemble and various demonstrators gather. Secret Service agents guard the White House grounds, and U.S. Park Police are in charge of the surrounding sidewalks. On almost any day of the week, sawhorses and barricades may emerge in preparation for the arrival of a foreign dignitary or a presidential motorcade. Helicopters frequently arrive and depart from the White House south lawn, and the lights and cameras of television crews are never distant.

Across the street from the White House North Portico is Lafayette Park, which is surrounded by many historical buildings. In the center of the park stands Clark Mills' equestrian statue of Andrew Jackson. Guarding the corners are statues of four

Revolutionary War heroes, all of them foreign-born: the Marquis de Lafayette, Baron Friedrich von Steuben, Comte Jean de Rochambeau, and Thaddeus Kosciuszko. Around the park are a number of federal office buildings, two of which, completed in the late 1960s, were attempts to provide additional space for the executive and judicial branches without detracting from the historical character of the area. These simple red-brick structures blend well with the older buildings nearby.

To the west of the White House stands the most flamboyant of the various structures built to accommodate a growing executive staff—the Old Executive Office Building, originally called the State, War, and Navy Department building. The architect was Alfred Mullett. Commissioned by President Grant in 1871, the building took 17 years to complete. Its style, French Second Empire, utilized mansard roofs, and its massive bulk and hundreds of window pediments and columns led many observers to regard it as a Gilded Age monstrosity. However, more recent revivals of Victorian-era styles have endowed the building with a kind of respectability. Government commissions as late as the 1950s recommended its demolition, but the tide turned in the early '60s, and the building was restored. In its lavish recesses have worked dozens of notable statesmen.

Across the street from the Old Executive Office Building is Blair House, built in 1810 by Joseph Lovell and afterwards owned by Francis Preston Blair, a journalist and an advisor to Andrew Jackson. The house is now the official guest quarters for heads of state who visit Washington. President Truman lived here while the White House was being renovated in the late 1940s and early '50s. To the east of the White House, blocking its view of the Capitol—one story says that President Jackson selected its location so he

Old Executive Office Building, completed in 1888, boasts more than 500 offices and ten acres of floor space. Some 900 freestanding exterior columns give the massive structure a fortress-like

would not have to look at the Capitol and his obstinate foes in Congress—is the Treasury Department building. This imposing Greek Revival structure was begun in 1836 and not completed until 1869.

The executive branch of the government is not restricted to the neighborhood of the White House. In the late 1920s, the area known as the Federal Triangle, comprising most of the southern side of Pennsylvania between 6th Street and the Ellipse, was given over to a massive project consisting of low-level, neoclassical-style buildings. Eventually the Commerce and Justice Departments, the Internal Revenue Service, the National Archives, the Interstate Commerce Commission, and the Federal Trade Commission would form a wedge between the Mall and downtown.

The buildings of the Federal Triangle contain a number of distinguished and at times

quality. Once the headquarters of the Departments of State, War, and Navy, the building now accommodates the Office of Management and Budget and most of the President's White House staff.

exotic interior spaces. The Commerce Department, finished in the Hoover Administration, has remarkable mosaic floors. The Justice Department, as a sample of New Deal aesthetics and Art Deco designs, is a wondrous place indeed. Prefabricated concrete ceiling panels by John Joseph Earley were done in a "polychrome" process which is now a lost art. Public works murals adorn the building, many with a powerful and almost surrealistic character. The Federal Trade Commission has metal gates emblazoned with clipper planes and ocean liners as symbols of modern commerce. Outside the building are statues of wild horses—unrestrained competition—held back by bold and muscular heroic figures.

Located within the Federal Triangle is the towering Old Post Office, a Romanesque-Victorian structure completed in 1899. Like the Old Executive Office Building, the Post Office was viewed by some as incompatible with the predominantly neoclassical character of federal Washington. The Post Office was recommended as a prime candidate for demolition until preservationists rallied to its defense in the early 1970s. The building is now being restored and when finished will include restaurants, offices, and retail stores.

West of the White House, along Virginia Avenue, executive branch departments continued to expand their quarters. The Interior Department building is yet another New Deal creation, filled with social-realist artwork. In the State Department building, located nearby, formality extends even to the conservative uniforms worn by the elevator operators. The former Civil Service Commission, now the Office of Personnel Management, exists in a high, glassy edifice that

typifies the architectural design of the 1960s.

Farther and farther, the federal office districts have expanded throughout the city. In the southwest quadrant, below the Mall, is a section of buildings housing agencies such as the National Aeronautics and Space Administration, the Environmental Protection Agency, and the Department of Education.

World's largest office building, the sprawling Pentagon houses the Department of Defense on the Virginia side of the Potomac. Inside the Pentagon, 17½ miles of corridors connect offices where some 25,000 military and civilian employees work. The decisions made here affect two and a half million members of the nation's armed forces deployed around the globe.

Amid the anonymity of buildings with names such as FOB (federal office building) 5 are two buildings designed by the famed architect Marcel Breuer. These are the Department of Housing and Urban Development (HUD) building and the Hubert H. Humphrey Building, housing the Department of Health and Human Services.

While some observers feel modern architecture exhibits a rigid uniformity, Breuer's buildings reveal how changeable the spirit of modern design can be. The HUD building, completed in the 1960s, reflects the sweeping, curvilinear forms of the Kennedy era—the era that produced the transcendent Dulles Airport. The Humphrey building,

ELAINE POWELL; ERIC POGGENPOHL, WOODFIN CAMP INC. (RIGHT)

completed in the 1970s, reflects a different mood through its blocky "brutalist" design. ("Brutalist" is a term employed by the architects and critics themselves.)

Provision for national defense and security has caused an unprecedented growth of government building, an expansion which has not yet abated. In 1942-43, on the Virginia side of the Potomac River, there emerged the Pentagon, a testimony to the will of America's people in their war against the Axis powers. This tremendous structure, with its legendary miles of corridors, all connected in a system of five concentric, five-sided rings, was completed in only 16 months. At one point in its construction, some 13,000 men worked 24 hours a day on the building. Legend has it that at least one worker was accidentally entombed within the hastily poured concrete walls.

The Pentagon is virtually a city unto itself, possessing its own dispensary, post office, and fire department. The building contains more than five million square feet of floor space—nearly three times that of the Empire State Building—yet no two points inside the Pentagon are more than a seven-minute walk apart. It was hoped that in the postwar world it could be turned into an archival facility, but the postwar world proved harsher than Americans foresaw. And so the Pentagon remained to become the citadel of America's defense establishment.

To the north of the Pentagon on the Virginia shore, the Central Intelligence Agency sits in wooded seclusion. Established by the National Security Act of 1947, signed by President Harry Truman, the CIA was created to serve as a centralized postwar intelligence system. Its headquarters resemble the quiet grounds of a college campus. Commissioned by President Truman, the CIA headquarters building was completed in 1963. Inside the central lobby is a simple memorial

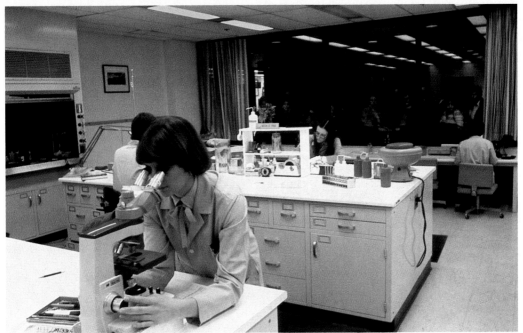

As visitors look on through a window, a modern-day crime fighter—an employee of the Federal Bureau of Investigation—analyzes a blood sample that could shed clues in a murder case. The laboratory occupies part of the J. Edgar Hoover Building (opposite), the new FBI headquarters.

to Americans who have given their lives in the intelligence service. Some of their names cannot be revealed even in death.

While the Defense Department and the CIA devote themselves to the task of confronting foreign threats to security, the Federal Bureau of Investigation is concerned with domestic security threats, with crimes of a national scope, and with federal offenses. A vast new headquarters building for the FBI was completed on the north side of Pennsylvania Avenue, opposite the Federal Triangle, in the mid-1970s. This building was named the J. Edgar Hoover Building, in honor of the late director of the FBI. It is open for the popular tours that feature gangster relics and marksmanship demonstrations, along with assorted exhibits pertaining to the history of the FBI.

With the completion of the J. Edgar Hoover Building came dramatic changes to the north side of Pennsylvania Avenue, changes that are continuing. In the Kennedy Administration, a number of federal and civic leaders decided the northern side of the avenue deserved renovation. A quasi-governmental corporation was created to revive the avenue, the Pennsylvania Avenue Development Corporation. Preservationists rallied to the cause of saving the historic Willard Hotel, which the early plan for the avenue would have swept away. The final plan, approved in 1975, called for more preservation. The area should include an assortment of offices, hotels, and residential structures when work is completed. Meanwhile, some of the historic buildings on the northern side of Pennsylvania, including the Willard, have been restored.

Monuments and Museums

Washington is more than just the site of the federal government; it is also a city dedicated to recognizing and honoring the best that our country has produced, in all fields of endeavor. Here are found monuments to momentous events and great individuals. Here are museums that catalog and preserve notable political, artistic, and scientific achievements. In many ways, Washington attempts to hold a mirror to America, to show us who we are and what we have accomplished.

Long before his death, President George Washington knew that his place in American history would be secure. Even while he lived, plans were going forward to memorialize his name with a fitting monument. Because of congressional delays, a National Monument Society was organized in 1833 to further the work of constructing a Washington Monument on the Mall. A design competition was held, and the winning plan was an obelisk set in a colonnaded base with statuary decoration. The designer was Robert Mills. A continuing problem of funds caused construction to come to a halt in 1854, by which time the colonnade and trappings had been discarded and the monument stood as the simple base of an obelisk, cut off at the height of 152 feet.

The Monument Society's efforts to raise money for further construction were set back by an episode that occurred in that same year of 1854, during the period of the

Citadel of justice, the United States Supreme Court Building (left) houses the nine men empowered with final authority over the nation's laws. Commanding the massive block-long front entrance of the Court, a vigilant figure in stone (above) holds a tablet backed by a sheathed sword, symbolic of the law and its execution.

Know Nothing party's anti-Catholic campaign. Until this time nations from around the world had donated stones to be incorporated into the monument. However, when Pope Pius IX donated a block of marble from the Temple of Concord in Rome, the Know Nothings stole the stone, probably dumping it into the Potomac River. The Know Nothing party later took over the Monument Society through an illegal election, further thwarting work on the monument.

Construction did not resume following these incidents until long after the Civil War. Finally, in 1884, the Washington Monument stood complete, its proportions significantly altered and enlarged by the Army Corps of Engineers. It once stood as the tallest structure in the world, and it remains a vertical focal point in a city of mostly horizontal lines. Today an elevator speeds visitors aloft, but stairs can be employed for the walk down during spring and summer "step

tours." Fifty American flags ring the base of the Washington Monument, and at night their flickering shadows play over the flood-lit surface of this memorial to our nation's first President.

At the western end of the Mall, on land reclaimed from the Potomac River, stands the classical memorial to Abraham Lincoln, completed in 1922. The designer of the Lincoln Memorial was Henry Bacon, and the sculpture of the President was done by Daniel Chester French. The inscription behind the sculpture declares that "the memory of Abraham Lincoln is enshrined forever," not only in the Lincoln Memorial itself but also in "the hearts of the people." This inscription is flanked by quotations of the President, including the Gettysburg Address and the Second Inaugural, which contained his eloquent pleas for "malice toward none" and "charity for all."

South of the Mall, by the Potomac inlet known as the Tidal Basin, is the Jefferson Memorial, designed by John Russell Pope and completed in 1942. The Pantheon-style structure echoes the design Jefferson used for the Rotunda at the University of Virginia and for his own home, Monticello. The bronze statue of Jefferson is the work of Rudolph Evans. Around the figure of Jefferson, the author of the Declaration of Independence and the nation's third President, are marble panels bearing passages from his writings. A circular frieze is inscribed with a passage from a letter to Benjamin Rush in 1800: "I have sworn upon the altar of God eternal hostility against every form of tyranny over the mind of man."

When the design and location of the Jefferson Memorial were first announced, they were greeted with criticism. One opponent said that the memorial's location on the Tidal Basin would block the view of the Potomac River valley from the White House, and thus destroy an important element of

L'Enfant's design. Other critics were displeased that several of the capital's prized Japanese cherry trees would have to be cut to make room for the memorial. When construction finally began in 1939, workers arriving at the Tidal Basin site found several protestors had chained themselves to the trees. Yet when the formal dedication of the Jefferson Memorial took place in 1943, the public was enthusiastic in its acceptance of the structure.

In the Potomac is an island known, at various times, as Mason's and as Analostan. It now bears the name of Theodore Roosevelt and features a statue of TR. The island, accessible by a footbridge, has a system of nature trails commemorating Roosevelt's lifelong support of conservation.

A drive across Memorial Bridge leads to Arlington National Cemetery, the largest of the burial grounds for America's honored dead. On a hillside overlooking the Potomac, below the home of Robert E. Lee—Arlington House—rows upon rows of markers offer a mute but powerful display of the price of maintaining and defending freedom. Occupied by the Union Army in the Civil War, the grounds were destined to serve as the final resting place for soldiers from each of America's wars, along with a number of statesmen and other leaders. Few who witnessed it will ever forget the day a nation said farewell here to President John F. Kennedy in 1963. His grave, marked by an eternal flame, is visited by thousands every year. Kennedy's assassinated brother, Robert, is buried nearby.

North of the Arlington Cemetery is the Marine Corps War Memorial, better known as the Iwo Jima statue. Dedicated to the memory of all Marines who have died in the service of America, the statue was designed by Horace W. Peaslee and executed by sculptor Felix de Weldon. It is based on a news photograph taken by Joe Rosenthal showing the capture of Mount Suribachi on the

Shimmering ribbon of water nearly 2,000 feet long, the Reflecting Pool mirrors the distant Washington Monument. In the foreground rises the imposing Lincoln Memorial. The Reflecting Pool has become a popular year-round recreation site—used in warm weather for model sailboat races and in winter, when the ice freezes thick enough, for skating.

Depicting a relaxed but resolute Abraham Lincoln, the statue below portrays the martyred President as he appeared during the Civil War. The marble figure gazes from the Lincoln Memorial (right). Resembling a Greek temple, the memorial reflects dignity and strength— traits of the man it honors.

ADAM WOOLFITT; STEPHEN ST. JOHN (RIGHT)

island of Iwo Jima in World War II. A newer monument to America's war dead is the Vietnam Veterans Memorial. Located near the Lincoln Memorial, it is a simple design in black marble inscribed with the names of every serviceman who perished or was lost in one of America's longest, most agonizing wars. The effect of this unpretentious memorial is dramatic and powerful.

Of Washington's numerous museums, the most famous—and most extensive—is the Smithsonian Institution. Actually a complex of museums and other facilities, the Smithsonian is an unparalleled center of learning. The Institution was established with a $550,000 bequest to the United States by Englishman James Smithson, who wished to found "...an Establishment for the increase and diffusion of knowledge among men." Seventeen years after his death in 1829, the United States government accepted the bequest, and the building which now contains Smithson's tomb was completed in 1855. The architect was James Renwick, Jr., and the Smithsonian Castle, as it has since been called, is a venerable sight on the Mall, with its red-brick Norman-Gothic styling.

The Smithsonian Institution has gradually expanded so far beyond its modest

beginnings as to constitute a veritable scientific and humanistic empire. In addition to the Castle, the institution encompasses the Arts and Industries Building, the U.S. National Museum (comprising the National Museum of American History and the National Museum of Natural History), the National Air and Space Museum, the Freer Gallery of Art, the National Portrait Gallery, the National Museum of American Art, the Hirshhorn Museum and Sculpture Garden, the Renwick Gallery of Art, the National Zoological Park, the John F. Kennedy Center for the Performing Arts, the Anacostia Neighborhood Museum, and the Museum of African Art.

Other Smithsonian Institution facilities, devoted exclusively to research, include the Astrophysical Observatory, the Chesapeake Bay Center for Environmental Studies,

the National Zoo's Conservation and Research Center, the Archives of American Art, the Tropical Research Institute, and the Radiation Biology Laboratory. Not all of the Smithsonian facilities are located on the Mall, and some of the associated institutions, such as the Kennedy Center, have separate boards of trustees.

A tour of the Smithsonian could start at the Castle and proceed to the Arts and Industries Building next door, which contains four exhibit halls devoted to a reproduction of the Philadelphia Centennial exhibition of 1876. This assemblage of Victoriana can make for hours of delight and learning as you pass, for example, a 45-foot model of the Civil War cruiser *Antietam,* or a mammoth ice cream-making machine, or a small locomotive, all displayed in a manner befitting the beginning of the Gilded Age.

The Philadelphia Centennial exhibition fostered the Smithsonian's role as the Nation's Attic. Previously, the Smithson bequest had been used to support erudite studies, more or less to the exclusion of popular events and exhibits. But when the Philadelphia exhibition closed in 1876, its materials were crated and sent to Washington, where Congress appropriated money to house them in a new "National Museum" under the auspices of the Smithsonian Institution. This led to the precedent of federal support for the Smithsonian, as well as to the inclusion of historical and technological exhibits along with the original ones on natural phenomena. For a number of years the Arts and Industries Building was used to house aeronautical exhibits, until the construction of a new museum for that purpose. In preparation for the Bicentennial, the building was restored to its 1876 appearance and filled with centennial exhibits sent from Philadelphia a hundred years before.

Crossing the Mall, visitors can find additional technological displays in the National Museum of American History, originally titled the Museum of History and Technology. Built in 1964, the building is almost devoid of external detail except for narrow, vertical windows. The exhibits inside represent an intriguing collection of Americana: a railroad hall with a huge Southern Railway

locomotive from the 1920s painted in green enamel with gold striping; a maritime hall; an exhibit of the gowns of America's First Ladies; an interior from a venerated Georgetown confectioner's shop; an automotive hall with a sleek Packard phaeton and turn-of-the-century horseless buggies; the

HERITAGE: ADAM WOOLFITT (OPPOSITE)

Tallest masonry obelisk in the world, the Washington Monument (opposite and above) soars nearly 556 feet above the Mall. Completed in 1884, the obelisk that pays tribute to the nation's first President draws more than a million visitors a year. Monument attendants inside sometimes wear raincoats: The slow response of the cool interior walls to a sudden warm snap outside can cause "rain" inside the upper rooms.

American flag that flew over Fort McHenry when the National Anthem was composed by Francis Scott Key during the War of 1812; and exhibits on the growth of American industrialization and mechanization. This is *material* history, the look and feel of the physical past in the United States.

Next door is the Museum of Natural History, completed in 1910 and featuring a splendid assortment of natural history and anthropological exhibits. A huge African elephant stands in the rotunda, flanked by exhibit halls of dinosaurs, marine life—complete with a full-scale model of a blue whale—birds, and mammals. Upstairs is the Insect

history objects, such as elephant tusks, woolly mammoth teeth, and petrified wood. The Natural History Museum also encompasses the National Museum of Man, which features extensive exhibits of human cultures around the world.

Among the newest, most popular museums to be added to the Mall is the National Air and Space Museum, completed in 1976. The museum's 270 aircraft, 100 spacecraft,

Modeled after the Pantheon in Rome, the Jefferson Memorial (right) faces the Tidal Basin and frames the statue of the nation's third President (above). In addition to drafting the Declaration of Independence, excerpts of which appear inside the memorial, Thomas Jefferson founded the University of Virginia. He also won recognition as an inventor, botanist, and architect. The low, rounded dome and classical pediment above the front entrance of the memorial closely resemble architectural styles Jefferson admired and used when he designed Monticello, his Virginia home.

Zoo, where chirping, crawling creatures are displayed in clear plastic cages. Trained volunteers are available to explain the world of bugs, and visitors can watch them feed and handle some of the insects, including hissing cockroaches.

In the Hall of Gems, you can see the famous Hope Diamond, and the Discovery Room offers collections of fascinating items for inspection by kids of all ages. Here you can touch and examine hundreds of natural and 50 missiles and rockets attract nine million visitors a year. The displays are set in a huge structure. Substantial portions of the museum are exposed to the Mall through glass walls, a fact that both invites investigation of the scenes within and adds an appropriately spacious touch to the exhibits themselves. From the Wright Brothers' plane to the *Spirit of St. Louis*, a full-size DC-3, and the Gemini 4 and Apollo 11 spacecraft, the vehicles of flight are displayed in a setting that suggests a vast hangar. Use of the latest audiovisual technology is everywhere apparent, but especially so in the museum's theater, with its five-story screen, and in the Albert Einstein Spacearium.

Facing the Air and Space Museum, and next to the Museum of Natural History, the National Gallery of Art occupies two contrasting buildings. The older building was

Triumph and tragedy: Marine Corps War Memorial (opposite), also called the Iwo Jima statue, salutes marines killed in battle. The Tomb of the Unknown Soldier (top), at Arlington National Cemetery, honors all American war dead. Nearby, an eternal flame marks the grave of John F. Kennedy (above).

the culmination of a project begun by Andrew Mellon, who served as secretary of the treasury under Harding, Coolidge, and Hoover. For years, the wealthy patrician had collected art, and by the early 1930s—when he took advantage of a Soviet plan to raise money by selling artistic treasures from the famous museum, the Hermitage—his collection of Old Masters had become one of the finest in the world. Mellon's donation to the government of 125 paintings and 25 large sculptures served as the core of the early National Gallery collection. Mellon didn't live to see the completion of the gallery in 1941, but for years afterward, visitors still referred to it as the "Mellon gallery."

The building was designed by John Russell Pope, who also designed the National Archives and the Jefferson Memorial, and it serves as a lasting monument to the neoclassical style in Washington. The grandeur of the National Gallery is apparent to all who bemoan the sameness of many newer structures. Its look is reminiscent of William Thornton's original design for the Capitol Building, though on a greater scale.

The interior of the National Gallery

flows from a central rotunda, where a fountain with a statue of winged Mercury serves as a focal point. In each of the two wings is a garden court, and 100 gallery rooms contain part of the vast collection. In only three decades, this collection expanded far beyond the Mellon bequest; it encompassed so many paintings, pieces of sculpture, photographs, and books, that a second gallery was required by the 1970s. This second building

Retired iron horse, Old 1401 (below) rests in Railroad Hall in the National Museum of American History (right). A branch of the Smithsonian Institution, the museum fronts Constitution Avenue. Inside the four-story building, some 50 great halls exhibit artifacts from colonial America to the present day. Displays range from gowns worn by the First Ladies to machinery—such as Old 1401, one of ten relay locomotives used to pull Franklin D. Roosevelt's funeral train from Warm Springs, Georgia, to Washington, D.C., in April 1945.

was constructed on land set aside for the purpose in the earliest planning of the National Gallery of Art.

The East Building of the National Gallery, designed by I. M. Pei, was built on a trapezoidal plot of land. Aside from its construction material—marble from the same quarry used in the construction of the main gallery—the Pei design stands in stark contrast to the parent building. Asymmetry and thrusting towers with knife-edged corners form a building that bespeaks the spirit of the 1970s. It was opened to the public in 1978 and features additional gallery space and room for offices, storage, and an auditorium.

The Center for Advanced Study in the Visual Arts, for example, has substantial office and library space in the East Building.

Another modern gallery on the Mall is the Hirshhorn Museum and Sculpture Garden. Completed in 1974, it was built to contain the collection of modern art assembled by the self-made millionaire Joseph H. Hirshhorn—a collection donated to the government in 1966. Some 4,000 paintings and 2,000 pieces of sculpture were acquired by Hirshhorn, with the collection concentrated on 20th-century modern art.

Near the Hirshhorn building is another facility built through philanthropy, the Freer Gallery. The gallery was designed in 1916 to house the collection of Oriental art assembled by Charles Freer, and today it holds one of the foremost collections of Oriental art in the world. Charles A. Platt designed the gallery to Freer's specifications as a Florentine Renaissance palace. Inside are exquisite objects from Asia and the Near East, along with James Abbott McNeill Whistler's "Peacock Room." The gallery has attracted scholars from around the world since it opened to the public in 1923.

Destined to enhance the Freer's attraction as a center for the study and appreciation of Oriental art is the newest and one of

Milestones of flight fill the Smithsonian's National Air and Space Museum. The diorama at left shows Apollo astronauts, in 1969 the first men on the moon. The Wright Flyer, the fragile biplane that launched the age of powered flight in 1903 (below, at right), hangs near the X-15, at upper left, the first manned rocket aircraft to fly six times the speed of sound.

EVERETT C. JOHNSON, UNIPHOTO; PAT LANZA FIELD (BELOW)

the most ambitious projects ever undertaken by the Smithsonian Institution. This project, a massive center to be called the Quadrangle, will house two new galleries, one the Arthur M. Sackler Gallery of Oriental and Near Eastern art. The second gallery will be an enlarged home for the present National Museum of African Art. The new galleries will be part of a largely underground complex to be built near the Smithsonian Castle. Scheduled for completion in 1987, the 75-million-dollar facility will feature a center for international symposia on African, Near Eastern, and Asian cultures.

North of the Mall, the National Museum of American Art (formerly the National Collection of Fine Arts) and the National Portrait Gallery are housed in the Old Patent Office building. Built in the mid-1800s, the enormous Greek Revival building stands on a square in the midst of an older commercial district. The National Portrait Gallery was established during the 1960s to house portraits of notable Americans, and its paintings reveal an interesting variety of personalities. The National Museum of American Art is the country's oldest national art collection. Its current location is appropriate: In 1841 the original basis for today's collection was housed in the same building. In 1906, with a bequest from James Buchanan's niece, Harriet Lane Johnston,

"*Uncle Beazley," a life-size fiberglass triceratops (above), entertains youngsters outside the National Museum of Natural History. Inside the museum, the world-famous Hope Diamond (right) dazzles visitors with 45.5 carats of rare deep-blue beauty.*

the expanded collection was designated the National Gallery of Art, a name it lost to the Andrew Mellon collection in 1937.

To the west, close to the White House and facing the Old Executive Office Building, the Renwick Gallery serves as a branch of the National Museum of American Art. It is devoted mostly to exhibits of American design, crafts, and decorative arts. The gallery was designed in 1859 by James Renwick, the same architect who designed the Smithsonian Castle. It was built for William Wilson Corcoran, yet another philanthropic collector of art who sought to establish a public museum. Originally the home of the Corcoran Gallery of Art, the building was designed in the French Second Empire style. Like many other 19th-century structures, the building was a candidate for demolition until plans for its restoration were initiated in the Johnson Administration. It stands today as a distinguished presence in the neighborhood of Lafayette Park.

In 1897, the Corcoran Gallery moved to its present location on 17th Street at New York Avenue, N.W. Its current building was designed in the Beaux Arts style. Except for the W. A. Clark Collection and the Walker Collection of French Impressionism, the Corcoran specializes in American painting and sculpture. It also houses a distinguished school of art. Farther uptown, a noteworthy gallery was established by the wealthy collector Duncan Phillips. The Phillips Collection was created in 1921 as a museum of modern art, though Phillips extended the designation "modern" to encompass the work of daring spirits from previous centuries, notably El Greco and Goya. In the Phillips Collection, one can see works from the most significant movements in modern art in an intimate setting.

Across from the Mall is an institution whose importance to researchers is close to that of the Library of Congress. Serving as a focal point for historical research, the

Eight-ton African bush elephant—the largest known specimen ever displayed—dominates the rotunda of the National Museum of Natural History. The museum holds a collection of some 60 million items from the world of nature as well as exhibits relating to diverse human cultures.

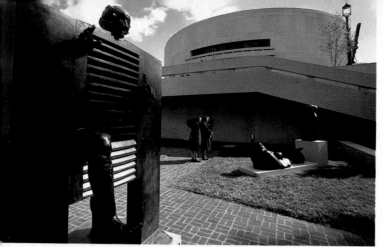

Sculpture garden of the Hirshhorn Museum covers more than an acre on the Mall (below). Some 75 figures adorn the outdoor gallery. Beyond the compact energy of the French sculpture "Man Pushing the Door" (left) rise the circular walls of the Hirshhorn. The building provides a showcase for about 6,000 works of sculpture and painting.

National Archives is also an exhibition hall for the fundamental documents of our nation's heritage—the Declaration of Independence, the Constitution, and the Bill of Rights. Designed by John Russell Pope and completed in 1935, the National Archives building is a massive-looking component of the neoclassical Federal Triangle. At its entrances on Constitution Avenue, facing the Mall, a sweeping flight of steps leads up to magnificent bronze doors, which many people believe to be the largest in the world.

On Pennsylvania Avenue, the research entrance of the National Archives leads to the working chambers of the building: the reading rooms where citizens can trace their genealogies or pursue research, using public records. Twenty-one floors of storage areas and stacks lie within the building, and in these restricted chambers, which the public rarely sees, are deposited the records of the government back to the Continental

Twilight bathes the East Building of the National Gallery of Art. Opened in 1978, the angular structure was built on one of the last unused sites in the original city plan. The sheer tower at left edges Pennsylvania Avenue, within sight of the Capitol. Inside the East Building (above, right)

Congress, records that include a copy of every act of Congress and almost every treaty. The most valuable records are stored in a locked vault. There, bound in great canvas-backed volumes, are the grand sheets of parchment signed by Washington, Adams, and Jefferson, along with treaties signed by kings, queens, and emperors.

A site of interest to the nautically minded is the Navy Memorial Museum, established in 1961 and located in the Navy Yard in what was once part of the old Naval Gun Factory. The Navy Yard is the Navy's oldest shore establishment. The museum holds more than 5,000 artifacts, including ship models, paintings, uniforms, and battle dioramas. Outside the museum are other exhibits: ships' propellers, a diving sphere, a Regulus missile, and early ship cannons. Nearby is the U.S. Marine Corps Historical Center, with exhibits illustrating the history of the Corps from 1775 to the present.

Historical Homes

Among the more interesting sights for the visitor to Washington are the city's historical homes. Throughout the capital are houses representing every phase of Washington's history, many of them sites of significant events or the residences of noteworthy

a courtyard features one of the world's largest mobiles, by Alexander Calder. Dramatic bridges lead to the gallery's displays of modern art.

figures. Decatur House, at the corner of Jackson Place and H Street, N.W., was briefly the home of the famous naval hero Stephen Decatur. The architect was Benjamin Latrobe, the preeminent American architect in the age of Jefferson and Madison. Until recently, Decatur House served as the headquarters of the National Trust for Historic Preservation, and two of the floors remain open to the general public. Close by is St. John's Episcopal Church, another of Latrobe's creations, frequently called the Church of the Presidents.

On New York Avenue is the Octagon House, designed in 1798 by William Thornton, the first Architect of the Capitol. He designed the house for plantation owner John Tayloe, who used it as a town home. After the British burned the capital during the War of 1812, President and Mrs. James Madison lived at the Octagon House. It was here that Madison signed the Treaty of Ghent, which ended the war. The house is open today as a museum, and the American Institute of Architects Foundation sponsors tours, along with special architectural and historical exhibits.

Across the Potomac, on the brow of the hill overlooking Arlington Cemetery, is Arlington House, often referred to as the Custis-Lee Mansion. George Washington's stepson, John Parke Custis, purchased the tract of land in 1778, and in 1802, his son, George Washington Parke Custis, began construction of the present mansion. The latter's daughter married Robert E. Lee in 1831, and the Lees lived at the mansion until the outbreak of the Civil War. Union forces occupied the house during the war, and after a tangled court dispute the Lee family sold it to the government during the 1880s. It is now restored to its mid-19th-century appearance and is operated as a museum.

Other Civil War-era associations can be felt at the two homes of Frederick Douglass, the eloquent black abolitionist. One of these homes, at 316 A Street, N.E., is now the Museum of African Art. Once a private museum, it is now a part of the Smithsonian Institution, and its contents will be relocated to the Quadrangle upon completion of the new facility. It is the only major American museum devoted exclusively to the art and design heritage of Africa. Another residence of Frederick Douglass is the house known as Cedar Hill, at 1411 W Street, S.E. Douglass lived in this house in his later life, and his personal library is preserved in this museum, christened the Frederick Douglass Home.

Another notable residence is the house where Woodrow Wilson lived during the three years before his death, after leaving the White House. The Woodrow Wilson House, at 2340 S Street, N.W., was designed by architect Waddy Wood, who also designed the Department of the Interior building. After Wilson's death in 1924, his widow, Edith Bolling Galt Wilson, lived in the house for another 37 years. Upon her death the house was bequeathed to the National Trust for Historic Preservation.

Next door to the Wilson House is the Textile Museum, founded in 1925 by George Hewitt Myers. The museum encompasses two houses, one designed by Waddy Wood and the other by John Russell Pope. It contains 10,000 textiles and 1,000 rugs from around the world, displayed in exhibits that change throughout the year.

Close to the Textile Museum, at 2121 Massachusetts Avenue, N.W., the exclusive Cosmos Club has its headquarters in the former home of Sumner Welles, under secretary of state in the administration of Franklin D. Roosevelt. The Cosmos Club was founded in 1878 as a men's learned society, its membership made up of professionals in science and in the arts. Members of the club have included many Pulitzer Prize recipients and Nobel laureates, and three Presidents.

Grand Salon of the Renwick Gallery presents a profusion of paintings in a setting that offers a glimpse of the furnishing styles of the 1860s and 1870s. At left, a bronze maiden lifts globed lights above tufted velvet settees called "poufs." Nearby, Bentwood chairs and a marble-topped table rest on a floral-patterned rug that complements the rich hues of the surrounding paintings.

Displayed under glass, the principal documents of America's foundation, the Declaration of Independence, the Constitution, and the Bill of Rights, lie in Exhibition Hall (above) at the National Archives (right). The repository and its regional branches store some 1.3 million cubic feet of historical records, a treasure trove for those who study America's past.

Across the street from the Cosmos Club is Anderson House, once the home of Larz Anderson, a career diplomat. The house is now the international headquarters of the Society of the Cincinnati, an order founded by officers of the Continental Army in 1783 and continued by their descendants. Except for President Washington, the Founding Fathers tended to look askance at the Cincinnati Society as a holdover from the European aristocracy. But the society survived, and the Andersons intended their mansion, built between 1902 and 1905, to be an eventual site for its headquarters. Anderson House today is a semipublic facility offering tours and the use of a library specializing in the Revolutionary War, as well as concerts and receptions for foreign officials.

In the same opulent neighborhood is the Christian Heurich Mansion. Better known as "Heurich House," it is today the home of the Columbia Historical Society. Christian Heurich, a local beer magnate, built the house in 1894 in Romanesque-Revival style. The mansion is a remarkable period piece, reflecting the Victorian styles satirized by *New Yorker* cartoonist Charles Addams yet now recognized as significant in American design. The Columbia Historical Society, which maintains the mansion as a museum, is dedicated to the history of Washington as a city and offers library facilities for researchers along with community programs of various kinds. Monthly meetings are held at Heurich House, where the architectural and cultural history of Washington form

ARCHIVES OF THE UNITED STATES OF AMERICA

PAT LANZA FIELD

the basis for lectures and slide presentations.

At the northernmost fringe of Georgetown is the mansion of Dumbarton Oaks, an estate with a lineage dating back to the early 1800s, when William Hammond Dorsey built a house on land previously owned by Col. Ninian Beall, who had named the tract for the Rock of Dumbarton, in Scotland. Subsequent owners made successive alterations, and in 1920 the estate was acquired by Mr. and Mrs. Robert Woods Bliss, who rebuilt it as the 18th-century-style country home that we see today.

The Blisses resided in the house for a number of years. During World War II the famous Dumbarton Oaks Conference was held at the mansion to lay the groundwork for what was to become the United Nations.

Before the war, the Blisses had donated the estate to a trusteeship administered by Harvard University. It now serves as a research center with programs in Byzantine studies, Pre-Columbian art and archaeology, and the history of landscape architecture. Dumbarton Oaks is active in all three areas, and its museum of Pre-Columbian art, housed in an elegant garden pavilion designed by Philip Johnson, is especially famous.

Landmark Structures

In addition to the government buildings, monuments, museums, and historical homes of Washington, there are dozens of landmark structures that add to the richness of the city. Buildings such as Constitution Hall,

101

ADAM WOOLFITT

headquarters for the Daughters of the American Revolution, are a worthwhile part of a visitor's itinerary. Constitution Hall is actually part of a complex of buildings occupying a square block and containing Memorial Continental Hall, Constitution Hall (the famous auditorium), a library, a museum, and an administration building.

Across town is a building Congress intended to become a Bicentennial visitors' center. Union Station is a stunning example of a turn-of-the-century railroad terminal. Completed in 1908, it symbolized the hopes for the new century during the era of Theodore Roosevelt. To save the station from demolition, Congress in the late 1960s authorized its adaptation as a visitors' center, a move suggested by the press but criticized by many as poorly planned. A huge depression was carved in the lobby floor to provide for sunken audiovisual displays, and dozens of mahogany benches were torn away. The building was saved, although today the visitors' center is closed. Plans to

reconvert it to a railway terminal have been announced. Meanwhile, a new visitor information center has opened in the Department of Commerce building.

Another splendid relic is the old Pension Building. The building is close to the area known as Judiciary Square, several blocks of federal and District courts. Completed in 1883, it is a memorial to the veterans of the Civil War, with its exterior frieze of military figures and its awesome, columned interior. It was the site for the inaugural balls of Presidents Cleveland, Harrison, McKinley, Theodore Roosevelt, and Taft. Today it houses the National Building Museum.

Along Massachusetts Avenue, N.W., is the area called Embassy Row. Between Scott Circle and Wisconsin Avenue, elegant homes combine with embassy and chancery buildings. Many of the embassy buildings were once themselves palatial residences, dating to the early 20th century. As wealthy Washingtonians moved to places such as Spring Valley, farther uptown, the homes were sold to foreign legations during the

Historical homes: Blair House (right), located on Pennsylvania Avenue, serves as the government's guest residence for foreign officials. Here in 1861 Robert E. Lee, before he committed himself to the Confederacy, declined command of the Union armies. Octagon House (below) functioned as a temporary executive mansion for President James Madison after the British burned the White House in the War of 1812. In southeast Washington, the library of the Frederick Douglass Home, Cedar Hill (opposite), preserves the memory of the famed black orator and newspaper editor.

1920s and '30s. Embassy Row continued to expand to the northwest with the construction of the British Embassy in 1931— where the noted statue of Winston Churchill was added in 1966—and the Brazilian Embassy, completed in 1971. Also on Massachusetts is the old Naval Observatory, along with the house that was built in 1893 as the home for the Naval Observatory superintendent. This home is now the official residence of the Vice President of the United States. Both the Naval Observatory and the Vice President's house are situated in a wooded, stately enclosure.

For years into this century, Washington was known as a conservative city in architectural terms, and with reason: The arbiters of taste were reluctant to break with the neoclassical pattern earlier set forth as the proper look for the city. Victorian design, much of it highly ornate, was as daring as anything seen here through the 1920s. During the 1930s dozens of Art Deco structures arose to give Washington a sense of the modern vogue that went with the age of New York City's famed Chrysler Building. From the 1930s through early '40s, many elegant

Set in Georgetown amid lavishly landscaped grounds, Dumbarton Oaks (top right) houses museums exhibiting Byzantine and Pre-Columbian treasures. Encased in glass, the Pre-Columbian jewelry and animal figures at right were fashioned from solid gold as early as A.D. 500. Two thousand years ago the winged object below may have glittered in the hand of a Peruvian dancer. A mosaic of water-covered stones handpicked from Mexican beaches forms the estate's Pebble Garden (opposite, lower).

FRED J. MAROON

ADAM WOOLFITT (BELOW AND LEFT); CYNTHIA B. SCUDDER (ABOVE)

Art Deco apartment houses were built along 16th Street and Connecticut Avenue.

In the 1950s, office buildings and apartments became more influenced by the stark International Style, the style of the functional "glass box," devoid of ornamentation. This trend persisted into the '60s. At the same time, several distinguished modern structures arose in or near Washington. Dulles Airport, for example, designed by Eero Saarinen and built in 1962, is considered one of the most beautiful modern structures in the world, with its sweeping roof and its virtual perfection of line. The airport remains underutilized because of its location 26 miles outside Washington, but a rapid-rail link has been discussed.

In town, the building designed by Edward Durell Stone as the headquarters for the National Geographic Society reflects the taste of the Kennedy era. The building was dedicated two months after Kennedy's death, in January 1964. It stands at 17th and M Streets, N.W., and its popular museum, Explorers Hall, provides displays of some of the expeditions the society has sponsored, as well as changing exhibits on a variety of subjects. Another example of modern design is the Martin Luther King Memorial Library, the work of the world-renowned architectural master Ludwig Mies van der Rohe. Designed in the late '60s, the library building is a classic statement of Mies' design philosophy of "less is more." Cool and black, the building has a quality of simple elegance.

In the 1970s, the architecture of Washington became more flamboyant. Much of the impetus behind this trend was the effort to escape from the "glass box" style. Wishing to make individual statements, architects designed structures such as the previously mentioned East Building of the National Gallery of Art, the J. Edgar Hoover Building, and the new Washington Convention Center, located several blocks north of the FBI headquarters. A more understated "post-modernist" architectural theme is being established in the red-brick apartment houses and offices recently completed at the western-most section of downtown Washington. The Thurman Arnold Building, at New Hampshire Avenue and M Street, N.W., is a good example of this simpler style.

Throughout the Washington area are numerous hotels and restaurants that cater to the needs of an international metropolis. Among the grand old hotels is the Willard, around the corner from the White House on Pennsylvania Avenue. Along 16th Street are a number of fine older hotels, such as the Hay-Adams, the Sheraton-Carlton, and the Jefferson. Meanwhile, tremendous modern structures, such as the Washington Hilton and the Sheraton Washington, are located on or near Connecticut Avenue, a major north-south thoroughfare. Also near Connecticut Avenue is the Shoreham Hotel, which opened in 1930 and was recently renovated.

Theaters also abound in Washington, much to the benefit of its cultural life. The National Theatre, at 1321 E Street, N.W., is the oldest continuously operated theater in the city, founded in 1835. It was recently saved in the ongoing renovation of the north side of Pennsylvania Avenue, which E Street intersects. Around the corner from the National is the Warner Theatre, a former vaudeville palace dating to the early 1920s that features concerts and musical reviews.

The John F. Kennedy Center for the Performing Arts—popularly known as the Kennedy Center—is a vast marble structure overlooking the Potomac River near the area called Foggy Bottom. Though the center had been planned for years, upon the death of President Kennedy in 1963 it was dedicated to his memory. Designed by Edward Durell Stone, the center opened in 1971. It is now celebrated as a place for the performing arts, where one can enjoy the finest theater,

Colossal Corinthian columns accentuate the enclosed courtyard of the old Pension Building. Galleries surrounding the courtyard lead to offices where from 1885 to 1926 payments went out to disabled veterans. Completed as a memorial to Civil War soldiers and sailors, the structure today celebrates the lore of American design and construction as the National Building Museum.

opera, dance, symphony, and film. The National Symphony Orchestra performs at the Kennedy Center, and the American Film Institute makes the center its home.

Housed in a new three-theater complex is the Arena Stage, at 6th and M Streets, S.W. The complex is in the area of the city's first major urban renewal project, a renovation now largely complete. Today this area is a busy waterfront district with marinas and several fine seafood restaurants. Arena Stage features a theater-in-the-round format. Its repertory company has often presented premieres of major new plays. Sharing the Arena complex are the Kreeger, a smaller theater, and the Old Vat, a cabaret.

A few blocks east of the White House is Ford's Theatre, which has now been restored to its appearance on the night that President Lincoln was shot. Plays are once more presented on the Ford's stage, and a substantial collection of Lincolniana is on display in the theater's basement museum.

On Capitol Hill, close to the Library of Congress, is the Folger Shakespeare Library, where a replica of an Elizabethan theater is used for the presentation of Shakespearean plays and other classics. The Folger, which is

Architectural splendor: On the District's outskirts, the sweeping roofline of Dulles International Airport (above) expresses the excitement of flight. The classically simple National Geographic Society headquarters building (left) stands at 17th and M Streets N.W. Modern hotel and office buildings border a spacious court and identify L'Enfant Plaza (opposite), a pacesetting example of urban renewal in southwest Washington that ranks as the largest nongovernment complex in the city.

"What, master, read you?" asks Bianca (below, at right) of Lucentio in "Taming of the Shrew," one of many classical dramas staged at the Folger Theatre, in the Folger Shakespeare Library. The Folger contains the world's largest collection of Shakespearean works and a vast collection of Renaissance materials. A scholar's desk (opposite) sits amid bookcases, hand-carved oak paneling, and wooden trusses that give the renowned research facility the feeling of an Elizabethan college.

JOAN MARCUS; FRED J. MAROON (RIGHT)

one of the foremost research facilities dedicated to Shakespeare, was made possible by Mr. and Mrs. Henry Clay Folger, philanthropists whose bequest resulted in the neoclassical building completed in 1932.

Far uptown, in the wooded recesses of Rock Creek Park, is the Carter Barron Amphitheatre, a facility operated by the National Park Service and leased to entertainers and promoters. In Vienna, Virginia, is Wolf Trap Farm Park, the gift of benefactress Catherine Filene Shouse. In summer and early autumn a wide range of entertainment is offered at this outdoor facility.

Colleges and Places of Worship

Among the many notable schools located in Washington is Georgetown University, founded in 1789 as the first Roman Catholic college in the United States. Its founder was John Carroll, the first American bishop and first Archbishop of Baltimore. It is situated on land overlooking the Potomac, and the spires of its Healy Building are clearly visible from the Virginia shore.

Another center of learning is the Catholic University of America, located on a tract of 190 acres at one of the highest points in Northeast Washington, along Michigan Avenue. The university was founded in the late 1880s as the national university of the Catholic Church in America. Today it is open to people of all denominations and creeds. The dominant feature of the campus of Catholic University is the Shrine of the Immaculate Conception, a church begun in 1920 whose splendor equals that of many churches in Europe. Its multicolored dome is now a familiar landmark. Close by is Trinity College, a

Memorial on the Potomac: The John F. Kennedy Center for the Performing Arts (right) encloses four theaters that spotlight the world's finest entertainers. Crystal chandeliers accent the Grand Foyer (above), while in the Concert Hall (top) ceiling hexagons and lavish use of wood in the walls and floor ensure the acoustic fidelity of musical performances, such as this by the National Symphony Orchestra.

women's college located at Michigan Avenue and Harewood Road, N.E., which was founded in 1897 by the Sisters of Notre Dame de Namur.

In the heart of the city is George Washington University, a school offering the vibrancy of a college campus in an urban setting. The institution dates to the establishment of a "Columbian College" in 1821, which became the Columbian University in 1873 and George Washington University in 1904. Its facilities span some 19 blocks of the western downtown area, near the site suggested for a national university by George Washington.

Located farther uptown, by Ward Circle on Massachusetts Avenue, N.W., is the campus of American University, a liberal arts university founded as a Methodist school in 1893 by the Methodist Bishop John Fletcher Hurst. Today the school is independent, although related to the United Methodist Church. American University is one of the most international campuses in Washington, where students from around the world converge.

Howard University, founded in 1867 as a black seminary, was named in honor of Oliver Otis Howard, a Civil War general who demonstrated concern for the plight of minorities. Soon after its founding, Howard was chartered as a university open to all races, though its student body remains mostly black.

Also located in Washington are Gallaudet College, an institution dating to 1857 dedicated to the higher education of the deaf, and the University of the District of Columbia, a newer school with several campuses. To the northeast of the city is the University of Maryland, a huge institution in College Park. In northern Virginia is the campus of George Mason University, and a number of community colleges are spread throughout suburban areas in both states.

Lofty steeple of Founders Library (below) looks over the campus of Howard University, one of the nation's foremost institutions of black education. On the grounds of Georgetown University (opposite), a bronze statue honors Bishop John Carroll, who founded the school in 1789.

Along with the Shrine of the Immaculate Conception at Catholic University, many other religious shrines and places of worship are found in Washington. Fifty-seven acres of beautifully wooded ground is the setting for the National Cathedral, a 20th-century structure built along 14th-century lines. The seat of the Episcopal Diocese of Washington, National Cathedral is used for worship by various faiths. A National Cathedral Association, with chapters throughout the country, has financed the still ongoing construction exclusively through private donations. The construction has been proceeding for almost 80 years, since the day in 1907 when President Theodore Roosevelt laid the foundation stone.

The project was originally directed by Bishop Henry Yates Satterlee, and the original architects were George F. Bodley and Henry Vaughan. Upon the deaths of Bodley and Vaughan, Philip Hubert Frohman was commissioned as the prime architect. National Cathedral today is one of the largest Gothic cathedrals in the world, and its profile—like an image from a delicate watercolor—can be seen from many points in the city. The cathedral's elaborate carvings, stone-masonry, and stained glass represent a tremendous outpouring of artistic genius.

JOHN CARROLL
FOVNDER

Gothic spires of the National Cathedral (left) rise 300 feet above wooded Mount St. Alban, one of Washington's highest points of land. Inside the vast church, soft light illuminates the High Altar (below). A temple for all faiths, the church enhances cultural life by sponsoring performances of drama and music.

SISSE BRIMBERG, WOODFIN CAMP INC.; WILLIAM S. WEEMS, WOODFIN CAMP INC. (LEFT)

Some believe the cathedral craftsmen are the last of a dying breed and that never again will such a work as theirs be possible.

Down the street from National Cathedral are churches for the Russian and Greek Orthodox faiths, respectively St. Nicholas Cathedral at 3500 Massachusetts Avenue, N.W., and Saint Sophia Cathedral at Massachusetts Avenue and 36th Street. St. Nicholas Cathedral, the work of architect Alexander Neratov, was intended as a war memorial as well as a place of worship. Saint Sophia Cathedral, designed by Archie Protopapas, was built in the mid-1950s, and features extraordinary mosaics.

Another place of worship is the Washington Hebrew Congregation, at Massachusetts and Macomb Street. The foremost Reform

117

Lamp glow glistening on fallen snow rekindles an early-day image of winter in Georgetown (opposite). Town homes similar to these once housed Scottish merchants who grew wealthy shipping tobacco to England. The expanding boundaries of Washington eventually absorbed Georgetown. Today the former colonial river port prospers with restaurants and numerous shops, such as the Victorian arcade at left.

synagogue in the city, the Washington Hebrew Congregation dates to 1855, and its original building at 816 8th Street, N.W., is still standing. The synagogue we see today was built between 1952 and 1954. The other great branches of contemporary Judaism, Conservative and Orthodox, are represented by synagogues such as Adas Israel, on Connecticut Avenue, N.W., and Beth Sholom, in Silver Spring, Maryland.

Located on Massachusetts Avenue near Rock Creek Parkway is the Islamic Center, popularly known as the Mosque. The Islamic Center was built in the 1950s to provide the correct surroundings for Islamic worship. The founders included a group of ambassadors from several Islamic countries and several prominent American Moslems. The architect, Mario Rossi, a student of Islamic design, previously designed a number of mosques in the Egyptian cities of Alexandria and Cairo.

Neighborhoods and Parks

There is still much of interest to see after sampling Washington's many churches, schools, and other public attractions. A rich variety of neighborhoods and parks significantly adds to the city's character. Downtown Washington today comprises an office and commercial district surrounded by a predominantly black urban core, posh residences in Georgetown and on Capitol Hill, and peripheral neighborhoods reaching to the city's edge. From the centrally located federal enclave stretches an urban grid intersected by radial, diagonal avenues. These, of course, were an essential part of the original L'Enfant plan. With the Capitol as the central point, Washington, D.C., is divided into four quadrants. Almost all of the downtown commercial and office district lies in the northwest section.

Downtown Washington has been undergoing a development boom of gigantic proportions. Those returning here after an absence of a few years are often amazed at the changes they notice. The most extensive changes have occurred in the western portion of the downtown area, mostly along the east-west span of K Street between Washington Circle and Connecticut Avenue. Block after block of older structures has been torn down to make room for modern office buildings. To the east, the older financial

*F*ifty-five-thousand-seat
Robert F. Kennedy
Stadium (left) offers public
events ranging from rock
concerts to the home games
of the 1983 Super Bowl
champion Washington
Redskins. A modern
marina along Water Street,
in the southwest section of
the city (below), punctuates
a revitalized sector of
restaurants, parks, high-
rise apartments, and
federal office buildings.

HAROLD FLECKNOE, UNIPHOTO; DICK DURRANCE II, WOODFIN CAMP INC. (BELOW)

and shopping districts retain their character. But the building boom continues, and plans for further development are being intensively reviewed.

Slightly to the north and west of the downtown office district, around a bend in the Potomac River, lies historical Georgetown. Georgetown was settled by Scottish immigrants and dates to the earliest years of the 18th century, when the Beall family established a plantation in the area. In 1751, the colonial government of Maryland authorized the settlement to adopt the name "George." In 1789 it was incorporated as "George Town," and it retained a virtually separate city government for a number of years. Today, after some 50 years of restoration, Georgetown is one of the city's most elegant districts. Narrow, shady streets feature houses of Georgian, Federal, and Victorian character. Georgetown has also become the center of the youth culture in Washington. Bars, boutiques, and sidewalk vendors are now part of "the scene" along Wisconsin Avenue and M Street, N.W.

Just north of the downtown area, clustered around the intersection of Massachusetts and Connecticut Avenues is a world of the avant-garde: Dupont Circle, an area whose ambience is as near to that of New York City's Greenwich Village as Washingtonians have yet produced. Close behind

*P*ockets of cultural pride flourish throughout Washington. H Street (above) marks the heart of Chinatown, where a fantasy lion (right) summons good fortune. Below, dancers samba through Adams-Morgan, a northwest community that annually celebrates its heritage at the Hispanic-American Festival. Bright embroidered flowers on Krakowski costumes (opposite)—a regional dress of Poland—usher in spring at Dupont Circle.

is the area known as Adams-Morgan, in the region of Calvert Street and Kalorama Road between Connecticut Avenue and 16th Street, an independent and multi-ethnic neighborhood. A Latin American character is evident throughout the area, although nearly the entire economic, social, racial, and cultural spectrum of Washington is represented here. Comparable in its distinct ethnic flavor, though less bohemian than Adams-Morgan, is the small Chinese district in the northern-central section of downtown. Here during the Chinese New Year festivities, the streets are alive with color as members of the community parade in traditional costumes.

Blacks have comprised the majority of Washingtonians for some 20 years. Black families predominate in the upper urban core and in large areas of the northeast and

ADAM WOOLFITT; MAX HIRSHFELD, UNIPHOTO (BELOW, LEFT); PAT LANZA FIELD (BELOW, RIGHT)

Carefree bicyclists cool bare feet in Rock Creek Park (above). The 1,800-acre woodland tract provides a retreat from city bustle. It also encloses the National Zoological Park (opposite, far left), home of Hsing-Hsing (left), one of a pair of giant pandas given to the United States by the People's Republic of China.

southeast. A substantial and growing black middle class has existed for years in upper northwest Washington and throughout the northeast section. Once a segregated city, Washington now reflects the black presence throughout its politics and culture.

One of the most pervasive and pleasant features of Washington is the city's abundance of trees and parks. Almost everywhere in the city are fringes of woods and tiny parks that make up a vast system. Nearly all of Washington's parks are run by the National Park Service. The most renowned formal park in the city is Meridian Hill, on 16th Street between Florida Avenue and Euclid Street, N.W. Both a park and a formal garden, Meridian Hill contains a terrace, grotto, fountains, and pool that combine in a sweeping array down a hillside.

The most extensive park in the city begins as a slender zone between Georgetown

and Foggy Bottom, then broadens into a thick forestation that follows the route of Rock Creek toward its source in Montgomery County, Maryland. Rock Creek Park is an urban wonder on the order of Central Park in New York, but much larger and wilder. Through the middle of town, north to south, runs a forest that remains as a clue to the original nature of the area. The land for the park was set aside by Congress in the 1890s, and subsequent improvements—picnic tables, footpaths and bridges, swings, and a few baseball diamonds—have not disrupted the woodland atmosphere.

A nature center in the park is run by the National Park Service at a site near the intersection of Oregon Avenue and Military Road. Close to the intersection of Beach Drive and Tilden Street is Peirce Mill, an early water-driven mill that has been restored to working condition.

In Rock Creek Park and throughout the city's other parks are remnants of 68 forts and batteries that guarded the city of Washington during the Civil War. Most of the forts are reduced to mere grassy ridges, or in the case of Fort DeRussy, in Rock Creek Park, a system of earthen trenches filled with leaves, and heavily wooded. Thoroughfares such as Military Road derived their names from their function of

*K*aleidoscope of activities makes the Mall, the Capitol, and nearby grounds lively places to visit. Above, Mexican dancers reel at the annual American Folklife Festival, staged on the Mall in late June. Spring practice in West Potomac Park prepares polo ponies (below) for the coming season. On the West Terrace of the Capitol (opposite) the United States Navy Band stages one of its weekly summer concerts.

connecting the forts. One of the best-preserved, in fact, partially restored in the 1930s, is Fort Stevens in the Brightwood area, at 13th and Rittenhouse Streets. Here in July of 1864 a Confederate attack was launched by a force under Gen. Jubal Early. President Lincoln traveled to the fort to inspect Union defenses. The story is told that as Lincoln stood upon a parapet, a hail of bullets erupted from enemy sharpshooters. Temporarily forgetting himself, Lincoln's guide—Lt. Col. Oliver Wendell Holmes, Jr.—grabbed the arm of the Commander in Chief, shouting "Get down, you fool!"

Surrounded by Rock Creek Park—and accessible on the Red Line of the Washington Metro, the city's subway system—is the National Zoological Park. This is one of the largest zoos in the world, and its original design was largely the work of landscape architect Frederick Law Olmsted. A great rebuilding plan has been in effect to modernize the facilities, adapting them as closely as possible to natural habitats. Among the most popular residents of the zoo are Hsing-Hsing and Ling-Ling, the two giant pandas received from China in 1972.

What the National Zoo is to fauna the National Arboretum, at 24th and R Streets, N.E., is to flora. Here on hundreds of acres is planted a beautiful array of azaleas, conifers, dogwood, and crepe myrtle. The National Bonsai Collection and Japanese Garden is a special feature of the park. The most popular seasonal attractions are the azaleas and dogwood in spring and the turning of the leaves in autumn; but even in winter the arboretum delights visitors.

The Mall itself is in essence a park in the center of town, with its splendid promenades. The Mall is also a site for seasonal activities, such as the American Folklife Festival during summer, and the annual Fourth of July fireworks display. Another feature of the Mall in summer is the Sylvan Theatre, an open-air theater on the Washington Monument grounds where events ranging from jazz concerts to Shakespearean plays have been presented. In all, Washington's many parks and wooded areas have helped the city earn its comparison to Paris. As anyone knows who has been in the capital in spring, when the cherry trees are in blossom and tulips blaze with color, Washington can be one of the loveliest cities in the world.

Sites Outside Washington

Surrounding the city limits of Washington are dozens of sites that reflect the overall history and culture of the capital area. Northward along the Virginia and Maryland shores of the Potomac River runs the George Washington Memorial Parkway, one of the finest scenic roads near Washington.

In a southward Virginia spur, the road becomes the Mount Vernon Memorial Highway and leads to the famed plantation residence of George Washington. Maintained for years by the Mount Vernon Ladies' Association, the mansion is open throughout the year for a nominal admission fee. The view of the river from George Washington's veranda is in all probability unchanged from the days of the first President.

Across the river from George Washington's home is a fort named in his honor. It has seen rather little in the way of military action except for a brief moment in the War of 1812. Spying the British flotilla, the fort's commander decided a strategic retreat was essential and blew up the powder magazine. The British then burned the fort. What we see today as "Fort Washington" dates to 1824. The fort served until 1945 as an Army post; the National Park Service runs it today as a museum and historical park. The fort is a military buff's delight, with its stone parapets and dungeon-like rooms.

Between Mount Vernon and National Airport is Alexandria, Virginia, an 18th-century port whose history is similar to that

Shower of fireworks blazes brightly in the Washington night. Each Fourth of July hundreds of thousands of spectators spread out for miles in all directions from the Washington Monument to view the city's fiery salute to Independence Day. Outshining the Capitol dome, the lights of the Lincoln Memorial silhouette boats on the Potomac River.

of Georgetown. Founded by Scots in 1749, the city was the home of some of the prominent families of 18th-century Virginia. Once a part of the District of Columbia, Alexandria was returned to Virginia in 1846. A backwater town from the Civil War to the New Deal, Alexandria—like Georgetown—has been "rediscovered" and restored in recent years. Its historical area, known as Old Town Alexandria, rivals Georgetown both as an elegant residential district and as a site for fashionable shops, especially those along King Street near the river.

Among the interesting sites of Alexandria are Ramsay House, the oldest house in the city and the headquarters for the Alexandria Tourist Council, on King Street, and Gadsby's Tavern, which dates to 1752, on North Royal Street. On King Street west of the city is the towering Masonic memorial to George Washington, containing among its exhibits the Masonic trowel used by Washington to lay the Capitol cornerstone and the clock from Mount Vernon stopped at the moment of Washington's death.

One of the best historical parks in the Washington area commemorates the Chesapeake and Ohio Canal, built between 1828 and 1850 to connect Georgetown and Cumberland, Maryland. Though the Baltimore

*S*unny piazza stretches the length of George Washington's home (left), the centerpiece of Mount Vernon, his 8,000-acre Virginia estate. At the secretary-desk in the study (above) Washington penned letters that helped inspire the founding of the federal government. The scullery (below) displays 18th-century china and tableware like that used by the gentleman farmer who commanded the Continental Army and later served as President from 1789 to 1797.

*F*lowers and fountains brighten Market Square (right) in Alexandria, Virginia, a historic port on the Potomac River. Bagpipe marchers (below) annually echo the area's Scottish heritage. Shoppers enjoy Old Town Alexandria (above), a refurbished waterfront district of shops, restaurants, town houses, and offices.

JOHN NEUBAUER

and Ohio Railroad eclipsed the canal, it continued to operate until 1924. The federal government purchased most of the canal in 1938, and the National Park Service began an immediate restoration. Today the canal and its adjacent towpath serve as a popular haunt for hikers, joggers, or anyone seeking to escape from urban pressures. Canoes can be rented from several establishments, and in summer months two restored canal boats ply the waters, led by mules in the care of latter-day riverboat men and women.

Past an area called "Widewater," the canal leads to Great Falls, in Maryland. A tavern here dates to 1828 and serves as a canal museum. A bridge that led to the Great Falls themselves—a thundering vision with redemptive powers for the psyche—was destroyed by Hurricane Agnes in 1972 and has never been rebuilt. The only way to see the falls is from a promontory on the Virginia shore, though the view is not as fine as the one from Maryland used to be.

Tours of the Washington area can encompass Woodlawn Plantation, built between 1800 and 1805 on land George Washington gave to his step-granddaughter, Nelly Custis. The plantation is close to Mount Vernon, at 9000 Richmond Highway. Also nearby is Gunston Hall, which dates to 1755

Gunston Hall (top), Virginia home of George Mason, exemplifies the life-style of a wealthy colonial statesman. Italian marble mantel enriches the drawing room (above). The quill at right hints at Mason's writing skill: In 1776 he wrote the Virginia Declaration of Rights, the model for the nation's Bill of Rights.

134

and was the home of Revolutionary leader George Mason. The plantation is located near Lorton, Virginia.

Day trips and longer excursions from the capital can cover a variety of attractions. Possible destinations include Harper's Ferry in West Virginia, the Shenandoah Valley in Virginia, and Annapolis and Baltimore in Maryland.

The Shenandoah Valley and Harper's Ferry are especially enjoyable in autumn, during the fall color. The scenic road called Skyline Drive, which runs through Shenandoah National Park, has many points from which to overlook the Shenandoah Valley, a region celebrated in folk songs and sea chanties. Harper's Ferry, the scene of John Brown's raid on the federal arsenal there and a strategic point throughout the Civil War, provides an equally impressive view: The town is built on the side of a slope where three states—Virginia, West Virginia, and Maryland—and two rivers—the Potomac and the Shenandoah—converge.

Annapolis, the capital of Maryland since the late 17th century, compares favorably in its historical background to Georgetown or Alexandria. And not far from Washington is Baltimore, a metropolis whose historical character, from Fort McHenry to the haunts of H. L. Mencken, is matched by the fresh vitality of a modern harbor city.

Visiting the many landmarks of history that surround Washington helps to put the capital in perspective. In the federal city itself, reminders of the past are all around, for here the past truly lives in the present—in congressional hearings, Supreme Court deliberations, and presidential messages. In its everyday workings the city has approached the great metropolis envisioned by the founders of the capital. A city alive with history, Washington serves to inspire both a due reverence for the past and a renewed commitment to the future.

Dirt farmer's cabin: Washing dishes in a wooden bucket, a woman at Virginia's Turkey Run farm portrays the hardscrabble life on a homestead of 200 years ago. Here 11 acres of living history show modern-day visitors how subsistence farmers lived in colonial America.

Touring the Capital

Visitors to the capital may wish to take advantage of the Tourmobile, a convenient and economical way in which to orient themselves to the city's major attractions. The Tourmobile stops at the Ellipse, Library of Congress, Lincoln Memorial, Washington Monument, Jefferson Memorial, Smithsonian Castle, Arts and Industries Building, National Museum of American History, National Museum of Natural History, National Air and Space Museum, National Gallery of Art, Bureau of Engraving and Printing, Arlington Cemetery, and the Kennedy Center.

From these stops, visitors can easily walk to other nearby attractions, including the White House and the Capitol. Riding the entire route takes about 90 minutes, and an on-board narrator provides a commentary on the sites along the way. Tickets are good for an entire day, and passengers can set their own pace, stopping at any point along the route. With a reboarding pass obtained from the driver, they can catch a later Tourmobile and continue the trip.

Driving in Washington can be a frustrating experience, even for those acquainted with the city's maze of traffic circles and one-way streets. Because free public parking is extremely limited in the capital, visitors are advised to take advantage of public transportation. Helping to tie the entire city together is a transit system under the Washington Metropolitan Area Transit Authority, known as "Metro" for short.

Metro's red, white, and blue buses are a common sight throughout the city. The Metrorail system, one of the most up-to-date subways in the nation, makes cross-town travel quick and convenient. Miles of the rail system remain to be completed, and crews continue to labor in caverns beneath the city and surrounding suburbs. But most in-town lines are complete, and Metrorail offers a welcome respite from traffic snarls.

Metro subway stations are marked by simple pylons bearing the letter "M." Escalators, some of them breathtaking in length, carry passengers down to batteries of farecard machines. Maps in each station and on board every train show the entire system, and station attendants or fellow passengers are always glad to help you find your way. Bus and rail schedules can be confirmed by calling 637-2437. (Note: Metrobus drivers are not allowed to make change, and therefore exact fares are required.)

Taxicabs are another means of traveling about the city. Cabs are usually easy to find during the middle of the day, but during rush hours the competition for taxis is intense. Washington cab fares are based upon a zone system, in which the city is divided into regions and charges calculated according to the number of boundaries crossed.

Before setting out to visit any part of Washington, you may wish to make a few telephone calls. Here are some of the most useful numbers: Tourmobile Service, 554-7950; Dial-a-Park (information on current park activities), 426-6975; International Visitors Information Service, 872-8747; Traveler's Aid Society, 347-0101; Handicapped Visitors, 426-6770 (voice), 472-5264 (TTY for the deaf); Smithsonian Institution, 357-2700; Weather, 936-1212. The following four pages present a listing of some of the most popular Washington attractions, along with maps showing the heart of the capital and the route of the Tourmobile.

On gleaming tracks a sleek train whisks into Metro Center, the major transfer hub of Washington's modern subway network. When complete, the rapid-transit system will include 101 miles of track. Metrorail renders the city's many landmark sites only minutes apart.

Washington Highlights

American University, Massachusetts and Nebraska Aves., N.W.

Arena Stage, 6th St. and Maine Ave., S.W.

Arlington House (Custis-Lee Mansion), grounds of Arlington National Cemetery. April-Sept.: 9:30-6; Oct.-March: 9:30-4:30

Arlington National Cemetery, Arlington, Va. April-Sept.: 8-7; Oct.-March: 8-5

Arts and Industries Building, Smithsonian Institution, 900 Jefferson Dr., S.W. Daily: 10-5:30

Blair House, 1651 Pennsylvania Ave., N.W. (not open to public)

Botanic Garden, 1st St. and Maryland Ave., S.W. Summer: 9-9; winter: 9-5

Bureau of Engraving and Printing, 14th and C Sts., S.W. Mon.-Fri.: 8-2

Capitol, Capitol Hill. Daily: 9-4:30; tours 9-3:45

Catholic University of America, 620 Michigan Ave., N.E.

Constitution Hall, DAR, 17th St. between C and D Sts., N.W. Museum open Mon.-Fri.: 10-3:30, Sun.: 1-5

Corcoran Gallery of Art, 17th St. and New York Ave., N.W. Tues.-Sun.: 10-4:30, Thurs.: 10-9

Decatur House, 748 Jackson Place, N.W. Tues.-Fri.: 10-2, weekends: noon-4

Dumbarton Oaks, 1703 32nd St., N.W. (museum entrance); 31st and R Sts., N.W. (garden entrance). Byzantine and Pre-Columbian collections, Tues.-Sun: 2-5; gardens, Nov.-March: 2-5; April-Oct.: 2-6

FBI (J. Edgar Hoover Building), 10th St. and Pennsylvania Ave., N.W. Mon.-Fri.: 9-4:15

Folger Shakespeare Library, 201 East Capitol St., S.E. Mon-Sat.: 10-4; Sun., April 15-Labor Day: 10-4

Ford's Theatre, 511 10th St., N.W. Daily: 9-5

Frederick Douglass Home, 1411 W St., S.E. Daily: 9-4

Freer Gallery of Art, 1200 Jefferson Dr., S.W. Daily: 10-5:30

George Washington University, 2121 I St., N.W.

Georgetown University, 37th and O Sts., N.W.

Government Printing Office, North Capitol St. between G and H Sts., N.W. Mon.-Fri.: 8-4

Grant Memorial, east end of Mall

Hirshhorn Museum and Sculpture Garden, Independence Ave. and 8th St., S.W. Summer: 10-7:30; winter: 10-5:30

House Office Buildings, Independence Ave. between 1st St., S.E., and 1st St., S.W.

House Where Lincoln Died (Petersen house), 516 10th St., N.W. Daily: 9-5

Howard University, 2400 6th St., N.W. (main campus)

Islamic Center, 2551 Massachusetts Ave., N.W.

Jefferson Memorial, Tidal Basin, West Potomac Park, always open. (Park ranger at site: 8 a.m.-midnight)

John F. Kennedy Center for the Performing Arts, 2700 F St., N.W., between New Hampshire Ave. and Rock Creek Parkway. Daily: 10 a.m.-11 p.m.; tours daily: 10-1

Lafayette Park, Pennsylvania Ave. between Jackson and Madison Places, N.W.

L'Enfant Plaza, south of Independence Ave. between 7th and 10th Sts., S.W.

Library of Congress, 1st and East Capitol Sts., S.E. Mon.-Fri.: 8:30-9, weekends: 8:30-6; exhibits in John Adams Building, Mon.-Fri.: 8:30-9, Sat. 8:30-5

Lincoln Memorial, west end of Mall, always open. (Park ranger at site: 8 a.m.-midnight)

Marine Corps War Memorial, adjacent to Arlington National Cemetery, always open

National Air and Space Museum, Independence Ave. and 6th St., S.W. Summer: 10-7:30; winter: 10-5:30

National Arboretum, 24th and R Sts., N.E. Weekdays: 8-5, weekends: 10-5

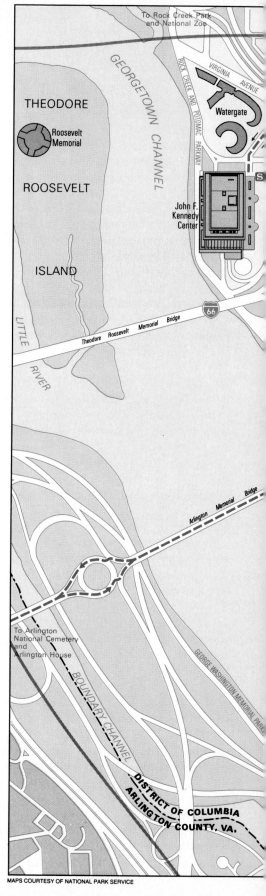

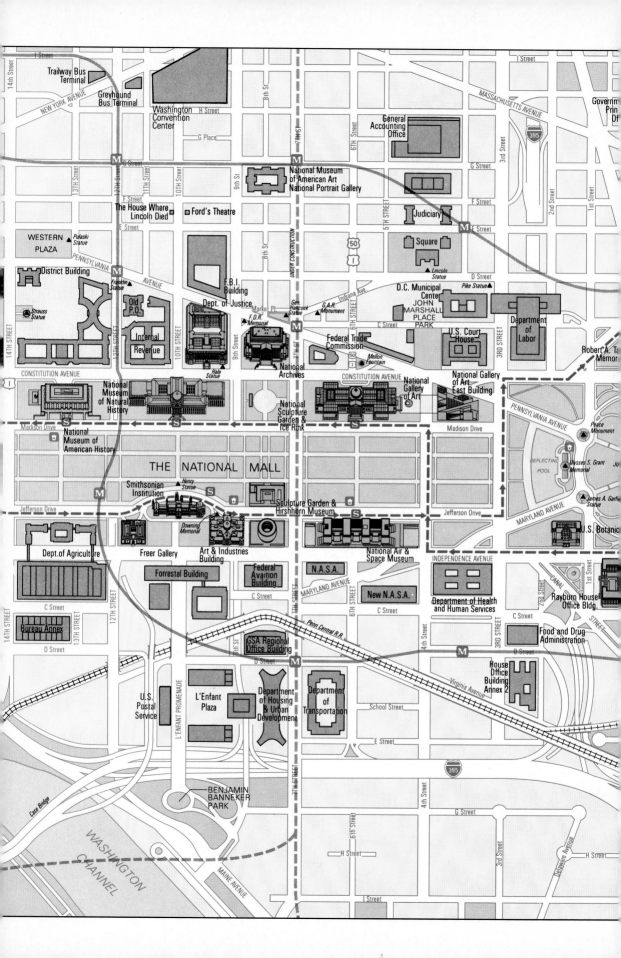

National Archives, Constitution Ave. between 7th and 9th Sts., N.W. Summer: 10-9; winter: 10-5:30

National Cathedral, Wisconsin and Massachusetts Aves., N.W. Mon.-Sat.: 10-4:30

National Gallery of Art, East Building, 4th St. between Constitution Ave. and Madison Dr., N.W. Mon.-Sat.: 10-5, Sunday: noon-9; April-Labor Day: 10-9

National Gallery of Art, West Building, Constitution Ave. and 6th St., N.W. Mon.-Sat.: 10-5, Sun.: noon-9; April-Labor Day, 10-9

National Geographic Society, 17th and M Sts., N.W. Mon.-Fri.: 9-6, Saturday 9-5, Sunday: 10-5

National Museum of African Art, 316 A St., N.E. Mon.-Fri.: 11-5, weekends: 12-5

National Museum of American Art, 8th and G Sts., N.W. Daily: 10-5:30

National Museum of American History, Constitution Ave. between 12th and 14th Sts., N.W. Daily: 10-5:30; summer: 10-7:30

National Museum of Natural History, Constitution Ave. and 10th St., N.W. Daily: 10-5:30; summer: 10-7:30

National Portrait Gallery, 8th and F Sts., N.W. Daily: 10-5:30

National Theatre, 1321 E St., N.W.

National Zoological Park, 3001 Connecticut Ave., N.W. Summer: 9-6:30 (buildings), 6-8 (grounds); winter: 9-4:30 (buildings), 6-5:30 (grounds)

Navy Memorial Museum, 9th and M Sts., S.E. Mon.-Fri.: 9-4, weekends: 10-5

Octagon House, 1799 New York Ave., N.W. Tues.-Fri.: 10-4, weekends: 1-4

Old Executive Office Building, 17th St. and Pennsylvania Ave., N.W. (not open to public)

Old Post Office, 12th St. and Pennsylvania Ave., N.W.

Organization of American States (Pan American Union Building), 17th St. and Constitution Ave., N.W. OAS, Mon.-Fri.: 9-5:30; Museum of Modern Art of Latin America, Tues.-Sat.: 10-5

Pension Building (National Building Museum), 440 G St., N.W. Mon.-Fri.: 9-5

Pentagon, Virginia. Mon.-Fri.: 9-3:30 (exit off I-395)

Phillips Collection, 1600-1612 21st St., N.W. Tues.-Sat.: 10-5, Sun.: 2-7

Renwick Gallery, 17th St. and Pennsylvania Ave., N.W. Daily: 10-5:30

St. John's Church, opposite Lafayette Park, 16th and H Sts., N.W. Daily: 7-5

Senate Office Buildings, Constitution Ave. between 2nd St. and Delaware Ave., N.E.

Shrine of the Immaculate Conception, Michigan Ave. and 4th St., N.E. Daily: 7-6; April-Oct.: 7-7

Smithsonian Castle, 1000 Jefferson Dr., S.W. Daily: 10-5:30

State Department, 2201 C St., N.W. Tours of diplomatic reception rooms by reservation only

Supreme Court, 1st and East Capitol Sts., N.E. Mon.-Fri.: 9-4:30

Sylvan Theatre, Washington Monument grounds, 15th St. and Independence Ave., S.W. Summer weekends

Theodore Roosevelt Island, Potomac River between Roosevelt and Key Bridges. Daily: 8 a.m.-dusk (approach from Virgina shore)

Vietnam Veterans Memorial, near Lincoln Memorial, always open

Visitor Information Center, Commerce Department Great Hall, 14th St. and Pennsylvania Ave., N.W. Mon.-Fri.: 9-5

Washington Convention Center, 900 9th St., N.W.

Washington Monument, 15th St. between Constitution and Independence Aves. Daily: 9-5; April-Labor Day: 8 a.m.-midnight

White House, 1600 Pennsylvania Ave., N.W. Tours, Tues.-Sat.: 10 a.m.-noon (enter at East Wing)

Index

Boldface indicates illustrations; *italic* refers to picture captions.

Additional Reading

Applewhite, E. J. *Washington Itself: An Informal Guide to the Capital of the United States.* New York: Alfred A. Knopf, 1981.

Bryan, Wilhelmus Bogart. *A History of the National Capital,* 2 vols. New York: Macmillan, 1914.

Duffield, Judy; Kramer, William; and Sheppard, Cynthia. *Washington, D.C.: The Complete Guide.* New York: Random House, 1982.

Equal Justice Under Law: The Supreme Court in American Life. Washington, D.C.: The Foundation of the Federal Bar Association, 1982.

Fisher, Perry G., and Lear, Linda J. "A Selected Bibliography for Washington Studies and Descriptions of Major Local Collections." *GW Washington Studies* 8 (May 1981).

George Washington: Man and Monument. Washington, D.C.: Washington National Monument Association, 1973.

Green, Constance McLaughlin. *Washington,* 2 vols. Princeton: Princeton University Press, 1962.

Leech, Margaret. *Reveille in Washington, 1860-1865.*

New York: Harper and Brothers, 1941.

Records of the Columbia Historical Society. Washington, D.C.: Columbia Historical Society, 1897-.

Washington: City and Capital. American Guide Series. Washington, D.C.: Government Printing Office, 1937.

We, the People: The Story of the United States Capitol, Its Past and Its Promise. Washington, D.C.: United States Capitol Historical Society, 1981.

The White House: An Historic Guide. Washington, D.C.: White House Historical Association, 1982.

Library of Congress Cataloging-in-Publication Data

Kennon, Donald R., 1948-
    Washington past and present.
    Bibliography: p.
    Includes index.
    1. Washington (D.C.) — Description — 1981- — Guide-books. 2. Washington (D.C.) — History. I. Striner, Richard, 1950-   . II. United States Capitol Historical Society. III. Title.
F 192.3.K46 1986   917.53'044   86-30887
ISBN 0-916200-08-6